What are people saying about this book?

D0814452

The following are reviews of this book's predecessor, *On-time, On-line, On-budget: Titanic Lessons for the e-business Executive,* written by Mark Kozak-Holland:

> *Perfect for any manager as well as IT management. Having had my own business, I felt when I read this book that the advice applies not only to IT but can be offered as helpful hints and warnings to just about business, big or small. [...] Mr. Kozak-Holland's book should make us all look at our past downfalls and ensure we all learn from them. This book works well on many levels's being entertaining, insightful and a fun read for anyone interested in history.* **(Alec Guiness, Calgary, Canada)**

> *A great analogy using the Titanic as an example of over-confidence in building and running a ship. If you don't plan to avoid "IT Icebergs," then you will likely hit one....and then what happens?* **(James Chillingworth, Toronto, Canada)**

> *Being a history buff, I was intrigued with a book that could link a historic non-IT project with modern so-called new wave online IT projects. I was not disappointed -- it clearly demonstrated [that] the more things change, the more they [stay] the same. The flow was pragmatic, thorough, and easy to follow. The language was geek free and informs readers on what they should expect from their deliverables and why they are needed; more importantly, why certain decisions are made and their overall impact on any project. In the end, the book clearly demonstrates, through the Titanic reference, that it is rarely a single decision that creates the failure but a series of smaller seemingly unrelated decisions that cause us to fail. Failing to plan does cause your plan to fail. I would recommend this book to any non-IT person, and any IT professional who is about undertake a project that involves Information Technology.* **(Tim Lalonde, Ontario, Canada)**

Titanic Lessons
for
IT Projects

Author
Mark Kozak-Holland

First Edition

Multi-Media Publications Inc. ❖ Lakefield, Ontario

Titanic Lessons for IT Projects
By Mark Kozak-Holland

Editor: Kevin Aguanno
Typesetting: Tak Keung Sin
Cover Design: Cheung Hoi

Published by:
Multi-Media Publications Inc.
R.R. #4B, Lakefield, Ontario, Canada, K0L 2H0

http://www.mmpubs.com/

ISBN (Paperback):   1-895186-26-9
ISBN (PDF edition):   1-895186-23-4
ISBN (Palm PDB edition):   1-895186-24-2
ISBN (Microsoft LIT edition): 1-895186-25-0

Published in Canada.

Library and Archives Canada Cataloguing in Publication

Kozak-Holland, Mark
        Titanic lessons for IT projects / author: Mark Kozak-Holland

(Lessons from history)
Also available in electronic formats.
Includes bibliographical references and index.
ISBN 1-895186-26-9

        1. Information technology--Management. 2. Project management. 3. Titanic (Steamship) I. Title. II. Series.

HD69.P75K69 2005   004'.068'4   C2005-905457-3

Table of Contents

Acknowledgments

This book has taken many years to complete. The initial idea occurred to me in 1994, and since that time I have spoken to many people who helped shape the book. I would like to start by mentioning some of the team members involved in the project that brought forth the idea; namely, Denis Cormier, Angelo D'Amore, Andre Beauchamp. I would also like to thank Sheila Richardson and Jill Batistick for helping transform the initial brief into a workable manuscript and Tara Woodman and Merrikay Lee for helping transform it into the initial copy of the book.

I am indebted to many Project Management Institute chapters for hosting the "Projects from hell – Titanic" speaking event. This led to many conversations with project managers who brought forth many comments and ideas about their own "Titanic projects."

I would like to thank Kevin Aguanno for helping pull this book together and for driving the initiative.

Overall, I am indebted to my wife and family who have been so gracious in allowing me to continue with this writing project at the expense of our valuable time together.

If you have any ideas for improving this book, please contact me via email. Your feedback can be incorporated into a future edition.

Mark Kozak-Holland
Email: mark.kozak-holl@sympatico.ca

Dedication

To my wife Sharon and children Nicholas, Jamie, and Evie.

Titanic Lessons for IT Projects

Preface

Most organizations have suffered through their "Titanic Project," a project that results in a catastrophic failure. Most Project Managers will admit to living through at least one of these in their career, and from my own personal experience I have seen my share of these during my career as a consultant. There are different types of project failures, however:

1. Some projects are obvious failures, particularly those cancelled or aborted during the project. The Standish Group brought this to light in their landmark "Chaos" report. (Research shows a staggering 31.1% of projects will be canceled before they ever get completed. Further results indicate 52.7% of projects will cost 189% of their original estimates).[1]

---

[1] Source: http://www.standishgroup.com/index.php

2. More critical failures are those projects that fail on or around implementation. The solution is already built and has undergone testing, but fails while being deployed.

3. The most critical failures are those projects that fail weeks or months into production, after the project has been deemed as completed. These are unpredictable, unexpected and by far the most costly.

In my encounters with this third type of failed projects, typically the project team has been disbanded and allocated to new projects long before the problems emerge. In addition, the operations group has been grappling with an unknown solution as they had been brought in much too late into the project to appreciate and understand the solution well enough to manage it adequately.

One of the challenges in investigating these types of failures is convincing senior level executives that the root cause of the failures is poor decision making in the project itself. Very often decision making was hampered by poor investments in the project and a focus on functional (rather than non-functional) requirements. (That is, *what* the solution does rather than *how* it does it.)

This also raises the question of when should a project end, and when can it be deemed a success or failure. As I began to understand these problems more deeply, I started to draw parallels from some of the notable disasters of the 20th century: *Titanic*, *Hindenburg*, Three Mile Island, Chernobyl, and space shuttles *Challenger* and *Columbia*.

Titanic kept coming to the forefront of my thinking as the volume of research material on the disaster is phenomenal. With *Titanic,* the 4 days of operations were chaotic and littered with mistakes: the breakdown in early warning systems, the failure to manage incoming intelligence, and succumbing to business pressures to better *Olympic*'s best Atlantic crossing time. Once the collision with ice occurred, the compromises in the project's design and poor decision making doomed *Titanic*. Most importantly, all these operational problems were rooted in the shortcomings of the ship's construction project.

My initial book, *On-line, On-time, On-budget: Titanic Lessons for the e-business Executive,* was created to help readers highlight how IT problems in operation or production correlate back to the initiating IT project. As a result, this culminates in a better understanding of risks and decision making, and assists in the better running of IT projects. Since the book's publication, I have had many conversations with readers, mostly Project Managers. The overwhelming feedback I have on the book indicated the need for a more high-level, shorter, less technical version that captures the essence of the *Titanic* story, which was proving to be the central feature. To respond to this growing demand for a simpler book, I have prepared the volume you are now reading

Mark Kozak-Holland.

CHAPTER ONE

The Story Begins

Most people are very familiar with the *Titanic* story from James Cameron's 1997 movie, or from documentaries on television. Typically, these focus on the last two days of the voyage and the last hours of the disaster itself. But what about the four-year construction project? Was it significant? What impact did it have on the disaster? What can we learn from that project that we can transfer to today's information technology projects?

Let's go back to 1909 and the business situation that faced White Star, the company that owned the fateful ship. (See Figure 1.1.) Their aging fleet of liners was grossly inadequate to compete with stiff growing competition. White Star embarked on a strategy to invest in new emerging technologies and create three super liners (two of which are

Figure 1.1: The infamous White Star Line logo.

shown in Figure 1.2). These were major investments as the liners were likely to be in service for at least 20 years. So for the designers it was critical to get the design right. They proceeded with a design strategy of luxury over speed where the ship's second class was equivalent to first class on other ships, and third class to second class.

To match the luxurious splendor (or the *functional requirements*) investments also had to also be made into *non-functional requirements* —everything that supports the functionals including performance, safety and capacity.

From the outset, no expenses were spared when investing in the latest emerging technologies for the non-functionals like the safety systems, which included a double skin hull (the bottom space divided into 73 watertight compartments), 15 bulkheads and electric doors, 48 lifeboats, and advanced water pump technology. However, as in many projects, a struggle took place within the project team where the success of the business strategy overrode other considerations.

One by one, compromises were subtley made in the non-functional requirements as the focus stayed on the functional requirements. Non-functional requirements were less visible, so this "corner cutting" went unnoticed. For example, the functional requirements for a spacious ball room resulted in four of the bulkheads not extending to the top deck, severely compromising the ability to self contain flooding. It was not only the business executives (principally Director Bruce Ismay) who were responsible for this but also the technical people—both the White Star architects and the Harland-Wolff ship builders.

By the end of the project construction stage, most of these safety features had been compromised. The height of the bulkheads was only 10 feet above the waterline in some places. The logical explanation for these compromises is that assumptions were made by the White Star architects that the "aggregated" safety features remaining would protect *Titanic* from whatever nature handed out.

By the end of project, the team believed that the safety levels were still maintained at the initial levels. So this set a high level of confidence for the maiden voyage (or

Figure 1.2: Sister ships Olympic *and* Titanic *in port.*

17

production). The arrogant view evolved that *Titanic* was a huge lifeboat. The *Titanic* project team made the mistake of believing the initial design assumptions, and not testing these far enough. Such was the confidence in the safety of the ship that by the end of the project, disaster recovery and business continuity plans were considered superfluous.

In short, the people "who should have got it"—the architects—allowed the compromises to pass. As the ship went into operation, a perception emerged that even if things did go wrong operationally the ship had enough safety features to protect it. This instilled a mindset in the crew and passengers that the ship was unsinkable. Why else were 53 millionaires aboard?

The ship set forth after a grossly inadequate "testing" phase, and enormous operational risks were taken. The ship's speed was steadily increased as it approached the ice field. Compromises were then made operationally as an ice detection test was fudged (see Chapter 7 for details), radio ice warnings were not passed to the bridge in a timely fashion, and a minimum number of lookouts were posted without binoculars. The ship's officers failed to piece together the extent of the ice field and understand the true danger as the feedback systems went awry.

Bring this story forward to today and there are many comparatives that can be made to modern IT projects, from construction right through to production. For example, there are many similarities with how IT project problems and issues surface days, months or even years after the project is completed and in production.

IT projects may be successful on deployment and pass a broad number of "standard" tests (system, performance and acceptance tests) yet still fail catastrophically when in operation. After all, only 25 percent of all IT projects are successful, a figure that has been continuously verified in various surveys.[1]

The success of IT projects should not be measured at deployment, but rather after the solution has been in production for a while and carefully measured. Metrics should be closely tied to the overall impact to the business. The *Titanic* story helps us better understand the relationship between functional and non-functional requirements, the interplay of compromises in the project and why things go horribly wrong in operation.

---

[1] Only 26 percent of all IT projects finish on-time, on-budget and with all the features and functions originally specified according to "Chaos, a recipe for success," Standish Group, 1994, 1996, 1998.

CHAPTER TWO

The Real Cost of IT Projects

L et us now go back to 1909 and re-examine White Star's business situation. How solid was the business case and did it cover the costs and risks adequately?

Today, before you commit to an IT project, you need to make a "go/no-go" decision on whether your "online operation" will be viable—i.e., the proposed IT solution has enough value to pay for and support itself and is not a "risk" to the business.

White Star's business case was very solid when viewed from a simple cost-benefit analysis. A staggering 75 percent of the total revenue was based on first-class passage. The three liners were viable within two years of operation. But was this enough, and did it cover the necessary risks and provide the adequate safety features needed?

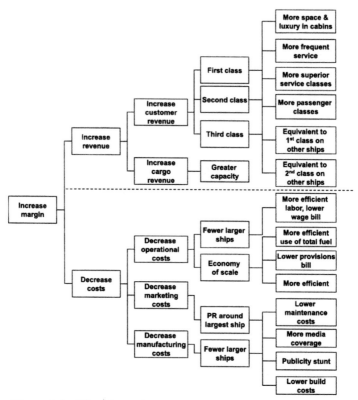

Figure 2.1: White Star's business case included items for both increasing revenues and decreasing costs.

Most IT projects go through a quick cost-benefit analysis to highlight their viability and draw on a three-year payback. A minority of IT projects go through a more detailed business case to forecast a return on investment and calculate the risks during the project and when the product of the project is in production (the online operation).

White Star, like any shipping company today, took out marine insurance that covered most eventualities in the

22

event of a disaster. But what could the loss of a super liner mean to White Star? Could it put the company in jeopardy? Was there a "repercussive effect" that needed to be factored in?

Today, very few IT projects look beyond implementation. IT projects have always carried high levels of risk, but the Internet has further increased this risk because it not only alters customer behavior and expectations for service, but also dramatically increases the exposure of the organization. You must give this thorough attention and consider the possibility of the IT solution being unavailable.

This is a problem because with the Internet delivery channel there are substantial "repercussive effects" that need to be carefully considered and factored in. For example, customers tend to be less patient and forgiving with Internet Web applications and will make a rapid switch to a competitor.

For White Star, the repercussive effect could be the consequences of loss of service, or in the worst case—a potential disaster. In September 1911, *Olympic*'s Atlantic crossing was cancelled following a serious mid-Channel collision with *HMS Hawke*. This also stopped construction on *Titanic* as *Olympic* was being repaired. A worst-case scenario like a disaster, where White Star was found negligent for loss of life, could put it out of business through the resulting lawsuits alone.

In creating a comprehensive business case for your IT project, you need to look at least a year forward of the online operation, with a simple formula:

23

*Revenue > (fixed costs + variable costs +
solution investment)*

In putting operations online, you are faced with the challenge of providing a 24/7 operation to your customers, partners, or suppliers. However, it won't always be 100 percent available. What kind of impact is this going to have, and how much unavailability can your organization tolerate? To get an accurate picture of ROI for your IT project, you need to factor in unavailability and its "real" cost into the above formula:

*Revenue > (fixed costs + variable costs +
solution investment + total unavailability
costs)*

But how do you measure the *total unavailability cost* and make it meaningful? Every minute your online operation is unavailable has an impact on your customers and organization. In that minute, you are not generating revenue or saving costs, and you can put a value against that minute.

To complete the calculation, you need to measure the number of times this happens for a period (e.g., a year) and the number of outage minutes assuming a 24-by-7 clock. A *User Outage Minute* (UOM) provides a meaningful measure and baseline to organizations. A UOM is based on the number of minutes one user is affected in an outage. So in the formula below, the UOMs are based on the total number

24

of outages, the duration time of an outage and the number of users impacted.

Total unavailability costs = Unavailability cost * UOMs

For each UOM, you need to calculate:

Unavailability cost = (average revenue per minute – absence effect value)

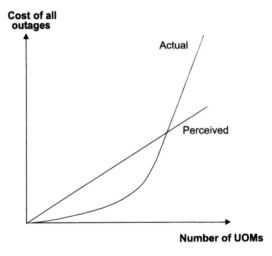

Figure 2.2: The cost of UOMs is actually much higher than most people expect.

However, with online operations, revenue is not evenly generated. More revenue is generated during peak periods. Knowing the revenue per minute for those peak period minutes is very significant because they are a lot more valuable. For example, with an online stock trading operation, the end-of-day trading period is the most valuable. The *absence effect value* is what it would cost your company if that minute of operation disappeared:

Absence effect value = (average revenue per peak minute + repercussion value)

The *repercussion value* is the ripple effect of the outage minute. For example, for revenue-generating online operations, this includes

- the impact of lost transactions,

- cost of adjustments and settlements,

- penalties paid for missing service-level guarantees,

- loss of customers and goodwill,

- loss of shareholder confidence,

- damage to image,

- brand-name erosion, and

- lawsuits and losses due to unfortunate timing such as outages during a peak sale period.

In the case of White Star, the repercussion value centered around penalties, loss of customers and goodwill, loss of confidence, damage to image, brand-name erosion and lawsuits.

Not all IT solutions have the same type of payback. A cost-reducing online operation includes the automation of paper handling, back-end functions or workflow processes. These have a different set of impacts, such as

- lost employee productivity,

- adjustments and settlements,

- additional support and maintenance expenses,

- penalties paid for missing service-level guarantees,

- loss of confidence in service, and

- losses due to unfortunate timing like outages during month-end processing.

White Star's business case payback period was relatively short, so the non-functional compromises were not likely driven by cost cutting. White Star failed to adequately assess the repercussive effect and incorporate it into the business case. Had it done so, the emphasis would have remained on investing in the non-functional requirements and eliminating risk as much as possible. After *Titanic*'s disaster, this lack of focus on non-functional requirements haunted White Star. The company was saved from bankruptcy only because the British government needed troop carrying ships when a world war loomed.

CHAPTER THREE

Design & Construction

Titanic's architects had many design choices, and from the outset they followed a business strategy to maximize passenger comfort rather than speed of passage. They never envisaged breaking the blue ribbon record for crossing the Atlantic in record time. This adjustment meant the ship could be built with a broad U-shaped hull rather than a sleek and fast V-shaped hull (Figure 3.1). This increased the ship's volume by 23 percent, resulting in larger and more comfortable first- and second-class suites and cabins that greatly enhanced the passenger experience.

Likewise, today you can copy your competition's approach or use new emerging technologies to gain an advantage. If you try something different, like exploit a niche in the marketplace, you may achieve a far better economic payback.

Mauretania   Olympic

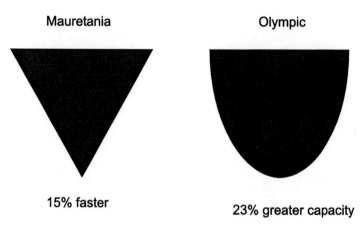

15% faster   23% greater capacity

Figure 3.1: Titanic's *U-shaped hull provided greater carrying capacity than competing designs.*

As part of *Titanic*'s design stage, the architects proceeded to transfer the business requirements into the functional requirements of the ship; namely, transportation and hospitality. The main functions included defining accommodation through cabins and suites, catering, recreation and entertainment.

Likewise, most IT projects transition through this stage relatively smoothly. Functional requirements are tangible and readily understood by both business executives and IT staff.

As mentioned in Chapter 1, the non-functional requirements are incredibly important because they define the operational characteristics of a system. For *Titanic*'s architects, this included reviewing safety, performance, stability, security, maintainability and the environment. So no matter what the specifications for the functional requirements were, the non-functional requirements ensured the ship could deliver the functions for which it was designed.

Likewise, on IT projects the non-functional requirements include availability (similar to safety), security and system management based on the runtime properties of the system. Other non-functional requirements based on non-runtime properties include scalability, portability, maintainability, environmental factors, and evolvability. Similar to *Titanic*, the non-functional requirements ensure that the system delivers the functions for which it was designed.

To determine the non-functional requirements, *Titanic*'s architects used techniques like a "shipbuilder's model." This 15-foot model, shown in Figure 3.2, provided a quasi-simulated environment for determining how the logical

Figure 3.2: The shipbuilder's model for Titanic.

and physical designs worked relative to the functionality of the ship. For example, was the power-to-weight ratio adequate, or how stable was the ship in rough seas? "What if?" failure scenarios were modeled to determine alternative safety features and their optimum implementation. For example, scenarios for the ship running aground or scenarios involving front-end or side-impact collisions.

Likewise, to define non-functional requirements today, there are a number of modeling techniques aided by computer simulation. The flow analysis model provides a high-level trace of each critical business transaction as it traverses the solution from end to end, as each component on the path is assessed for its non-functional characteristics, particularly availability. Another technique is to use this model for worst-case failure scenarios for single or aggregated components (hardware or software) along these paths. For example, the impact during peak transaction flows, or during a cyber attack. This approach is also known as *static testing* or a dry run, or walkthrough, as opposed to *dynamic testing*.

Titanic's architects had to assess the availability (safety) features, make investment choices, and effectively select one of four levels of availability based on the possible what-if failure scenarios. For example, the basic availability level was defined as having no safety features at all, where the ship had the characteristics of a closed rowing boat, good enough to operate across the English Channel but not in open sea. The highest level was defined as having a comprehensive set of safety features to include a full compliment of lifeboats (Figures 3.3), water pumps, and advanced features such as a double hull, multiple watertight compartments (Figure 3.5), sealed bulkheads, electric doors (Figure 8.2), a collision ram (Figure 3.4), and pressurized air to force water out. The ship had the characteristics of an ocean-going vessel good enough to make transatlantic crossings at full speed.

Today, you need to assess availability features and make investment choices. There are numerous techniques for improving the availability of a solution through software and hardware, and protecting against the five classes of outages:

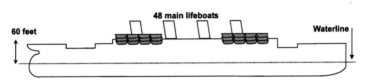

Figure 3.3: Titanic's *original lifeboat complement.*

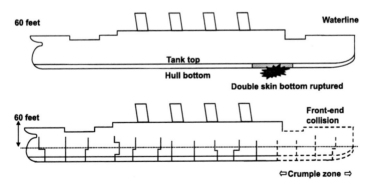

Figure 3.4: A double-hull design and bulk heads reduces the likelihood of a collision flooding the interior of the ship.

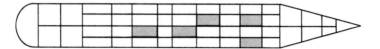

Figure 3.5: The ship was divided into multiple watertight compartments to contain flooding in case the double hull is pierced in a collision.

physical, design, operations, environmental, and reconfiguration. These techniques include everything from clustering to fault-tolerant systems to tiering, which enables "sideways scalability" of components and eliminates single failure points through replication and redundancy.

In the end, *Titanic*'s architects opted to go with the highest level of safety and incorporate all the latest and advanced safety technologies. After all, they were building the best ship they could based on the latest emerging technologies. However, *Titanic*'s architects started to make compromises to these safety features because of executive business pressure, notably from White Star Director Bruce Ismay who wanted to create the ultimate passenger (first-class) experience. For example, four of the bulkhead walls did not reach the top deck and were only 10 feet above the water line, to make room for a spacious 200 foot ballroom. Similarly, triple stacked lifeboats (48 in all) that would have obscured the ocean vista from the first-class suites were compromised for a single but much lower bank of 16 lifeboats (Figure 3.6).

Similarly, in today's IT projects hundreds of micro-decisions are made daily or weekly, decisions that are deemed too technical for business executives. Non-functional requirements are typically beyond the comfort

Figure 3.6: Titanic *sailed with only a fraction of the originally-specified lifeboats shown in Figure 3.3.*

zone of most business executives so any compromises to these may not be readily understood. Yet, they may have a major impact later, once the solution is in production and can affect the business itself.

By *Titanic*'s construction stage (Figure 3.7), it was almost too late. There was no comprehension that there was anything seriously wrong. Even though the ship's non-functional requirements had been compromised, the belief persisted amongst *Titanic*'s architects that *Titanic* was practically unsinkable. The broad hull design, the sheer size of the ship (50 percent increase in length over the last great ships built), and the aggregated effect of all of the advanced safety features and technologies set the perception amongst White Star staff that *Titanic* was invincible. *Titanic* could survive any situation, and so greater risks could be taken.

35

In this atmosphere, it is easy to see how the architects justified limiting the number of lifeboats to 16, the most serious compromise of all. Lifeboats were now deemed as an added safety feature, something useful if *Titanic* had to rescue passengers from other ships in distress. Of course, *Titanic* was never envisaged to be a ship in distress itself.

The perception that the ship was practically unsinkable was spread to White Star's marketing of *Titanic*. As the interior of the ship took shape during the construction stage, the visible lavish investments in passenger comfort implied that there was an equivalent investment in the less visible ship's safety and operational features. Rather like buying a luxury automobile today, *Titanic* was marketed to the public as practically unsinkable and this became widely accepted.

Figure 3.7: This photo showing the laying of Titanic's *keel shows the massive size of the construction project.*

Conclusions

Today, many IT projects are severely compromised in the design and construction stages, almost innocuously. But the impact of these compromises may not be apparent as any problems may not surface until days, months or even years after the project is completed and the solution is in production. Project managers need to ensure that as much attention is paid to the non-functional as the functional requirements.

Very often, the non-functional requirements are sacrificed because they are less visible and their importance is not highlighted to business people, project leaders or executive decision-makers. With hundreds of micro decisions being made weekly, project managers also need to aggregate the impact of these for the business executives to understand.

CHAPTER FOUR

Test Planning

B y the time the test planning stage started, the perception amongst White Star staff was that *Titanic* was invincible. In fact, this was used actively as part of the marketing for *Titanic*. As *Titanic* neared completion, tests were planned by Harland and Wolff (the shipbuilder) before she was passed over to White Star. Both organizations needed to be assured that *Titanic* would meet the conditions and requirements laid out in the contract. Testing gave the shipbuilder an opportunity to make any necessary adjustments and avoid the risk of financial penalties or having the ship sent back to the shipyards.

Likewise, IT solutions should have contractual obligations that should be tied to service levels objectives established earlier in the project. The business case determines the solution costs and the level of service required based on how much unavailability the organization can tolerate. Testing should assess how well the IT solution will meet these service levels and identify any gaps.

Planning typically consists of outlining a plan for several types of testing. For example, *Titanic* had to be operationally tested for seaworthiness, checked for stability and carefully assessed for weight and loading particulars. One test was the "incline test" that checked the ship's weight and center of gravity using a simple inclining experiment. It also acted as a check on earlier manual calculations. Other tests included the dockside trials that were held for the preliminary testing of main and auxiliary machinery. Formal speed trials were normally necessary to fulfill contract terms. These required achieving a certain speed under specific conditions of draft and deadweight.

Likewise, IT projects need to outline plans for testing the IT solution, and this needs to be done for both the functional and the non-functional requirements. However, the focus should be on testing the incredibly important non-

Figure 4.1: Workers leaving the Harland and Wolff shipyard.

functional requirements because they define the operational characteristics of a system. The testing needs to be dynamic, building on earlier static testing (or walkthroughs).

Many IT projects test functions at the unit level but fail to test the overall system parameters. This is partly because of the perceived high costs of simulating a service-delivery environment, so only partial testing is ever completed, which lowers confidence for a successful launch. Many organizations actually launch the IT solution with the view that any problems will be flushed out by the user or client in the short term. This is an extremely risky approach that might put the business in serious jeopardy.

In *Titanic*'s story, the sister ship *Olympic* played a significant role in the project as it compromised both the test planning and testing stages. *Titanic* was a copy of *Olympic*, which went into service in June 1911. White Star deemed *Olympic*'s track record adequate for launching an almost identical sister ship straight into service without extensive sea trials. The track record reinforced the ship owner's perception that *Titanic* was mission-ready. However, this only involved comparing the physical structures of the two ships and did not look at the readiness of the crew (people) or procedures (processes).

IT projects may make a similar mistake in depending too much on previous similar implementations and not completing an assessment of the business risk and technical risk of an impending launch. An assessment determines which tests are required, why the tests should be undertaken, and the test objectives and overall testing strategy.

The extensive tests performed should include stress, performance, regression, security and operational testing. This requires planning test cases for each testing objective: what is being tested, how it is to be tested, with what data, and what are the expected outcomes or results. Most importantly, these test cases should test the availability features of the solution. Planning should determine how the tests are to be performed, in what environment, and who can objectively perform the tests. For example, development teams should never test their own work; rather, independent teams should do so.

Olympic's track-record was not perfect, with several serious incidents. The first occurred as *Olympic* was pulled up the North River by 12 tugs and maneuvered into Pier 59 for mooring. The tug *Hallenbeck* was standing by at the stern of the liner, when a sudden reverse of *Olympic*'s starboard propeller drew *Hallenbeck* in and cut off its stern frame, rudder, and wheel shaft.

The second incident occurred while sailing out of the Solent at the start of her sixth voyage. She was traveling in parallel to the Royal Navy cruiser *HMS Hawke* in a narrow channel 200 yards apart and at 15 knots when *Hawke* suddenly turned hard and collided with *Olympic* head-on (Figure 4.2), piercing her outer skin. The damage was considerable: a gaping triangular hole around 15 feet high, 10 feet across, and 10 feet deep (Figure 4.3). Two of the largest watertight compartments rapidly filled with water, so all the watertight doors were closed. Even with any two compartments open to the sea, the ship would not sink.

Incredibly, no one was hurt as the second-class cabins that were sliced open were empty because passengers were lunching in the dining room. *Hawke* was equipped with a ram that absorbed the impact and lessened her damage.

IT projects must look carefully at the track-records of previous projects and their implementation success to determine lessons learned and understand some of the risks. With *Olympic*, it was obvious that the crew were challenged by the large size and the new technologies of the ship.

Following the *Hawke* collision, *Olympic* unloaded her 1,300 passengers and was out of service for six weeks in the Belfast dry dock as plating was replaced. At the accident inquiry, Royal Navy experts put the blame on the powerful forces of suction (known as Bernoulli's Principle) that were exerted by *Olympic*, which was seven times heavier than *Hawke*. This incident is significant because *Titanic* was to have a very near collision on leaving Southampton in 1912.

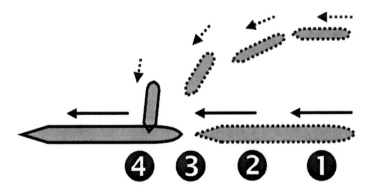

Figure 4.2: An illustration of how HMS Hawke *collided with* Olympic *shows how the piercing hole was made.*

Figure 4.3: Despite the gaping hole, Olympic *survived.*

What is even more significant is that Captain Smith, First Officer Murdoch, and Second Officer Lightoller were part of the ship's crew on both voyages. In fact, White Star promoted Captain Smith to command the flagship of the fleet as a show of confidence. The *Hawke* incident haunted Captain Smith, however, and he continued to claim his innocence by stating that *Hawke* had struck *Olympic*, and that the collision was the fault of *Hawke*'s captain.

IT projects should closely examine how previous solutions operated in service, taking particular note of any procedures used and organizations involved. Any failures or anomalies need to be closely examined through a post mortem and used as input to the overall planning.

Conclusions

Today, many IT projects do not adequately plan for testing that can prevent severe compromises in the solution when it is transferred into production. It is very likely that, with *Olympic* in service, White Star deemed *Titanic*'s maiden voyage as being low risk. After all, the two ships were nearly identical, and the ship's owners and crew were very confident in *Titanic*. However, no two ships have identical handling characteristics. White Star took a massive gamble in not planning for testing, and sending *Titanic* across the Atlantic with a skeleton crew. As *Titanic*'s project moved to the next stage, little had changed in the perception that the ship was practically unsinkable.

CHAPTER FIVE

Testing

When the testing stage started, the perception that *Titanic* was invincible existed not only with the White Star staff but also with the public. This, coupled with the ship owner's perception of *Olympic*'s solid track record, enforced the rationale that *Titanic* was mission-ready. As a result, *Titanic* underwent one day of sea trials in April 1912. The crew was eager to compare the new ship's speed to *Olympic*. This was in contrast to the *Olympic*, which underwent more far-reaching sea trials that included actual engine tests and adjustments to her compasses.

But what was missing from *Titanic*'s trials? Not only were the trials not extensive but they were also not considered critical. As a result, *Titanic* was not put through any complex handling maneuvers like "S-turns" that are used to get around hazards in an emergency. The officers also had very little time to acclimatize to the handling of the ship. *Olympic* was used as a test bed or yardstick for *Titanic*, and much faith was put in her track record. However, it is debatable how well the experiences learned from *Olympic* were applied to *Titanic*, especially when her track record was viewed so positively.

Figure 5.1: Titanic *passed her limited sea trials with little trouble.*

Likewise, IT project managers may make a similar mistake in putting too much dependency on previous similar implementations and cutting back on testing. The testing stage should be extensive and should closely examine the non-functional requirements that define the operational characteristics of a system and determine run time availability, security and system management, as well as non-runtime scalability, portability, maintainability, environmental factors and evolvability. The non-functional requirements ensure the system delivers the functions for which it was designed.

The business pressures for *Titanic* to go live were enormous. This was understandable, considering the large investments tied up in its four-year construction. In addition, *Olympic* had been out of service for a month in dry dock for repair because of the collision with *HMS Hawke* (Figure 5.2). This further delayed work on *Titanic*, moving her maiden voyage back from March to April 1912. White Star Director Bruce Ismay pushed the sailing date forward because he was convinced that *Titanic* was ready.

The lesson from this for IT projects today is to move into a launch schedule only according to pre-agreed plans, so

Figure 5.2: Another look at the damage Olympic *suffered during her collision with* Hawke.

that the organization (and more specifically the operations group) is well prepared and ready. It is important to assess any new business changes through a change-management process that carefully examines the risks, as in the case of an earlier launch date. Of course, formalized change management and control theory had not been established in 1912 so the ship was launched without plans for thorough testing.

To ensure a smooth transfer of ownership, Ismay decided he would be onboard for the maiden voyage along with Harland and Wolff's chief architect and key engineers. This was to have a dramatic impact later in the story.

There is a lesson here for today's IT projects — should Ismay have been on board at all because of his director's position. The captain of the ship is the key decision maker, and by introducing a director on board it could potentially usurp the reporting hierarchy of the captain and officers who worked for him.

With the staggered construction delivery of three ships, Ismay realized he had a marketing opportunity where he could make the case that each ship was an improvement over the last. In fact, this is a typical expectation of a technology oriented society. By beating *Olympic*'s best crossing time he could market *Titanic* as a superior liner. To promote this fact, Ismay published a shipping announcement in the *New York Times* before *Titanic*'s maiden voyage stating that *Titanic* would arrive a day early to White Star's published schedule. This was a publicity stunt; however, this was effectively creating a new Service Level Objective

(SLO) for *Titanic* without verifying it with his captain and officers. This proved to be fateful in pushing the ship to its operational limits.

The lesson from this for IT projects today is that SLOs should not normally come under the control of the business, but rather the operations group that has the mandate to run the system in production. The business certainly has a role in helping define what the SLOs should look like, but this is something that should be carefully negotiated and agreed upon.

In truth, there were no improvements to *Titanic*'s power output and speed over *Olympic*. Both were identical, apart from some cosmetic differences with some of the functions. Ismay was going to race *Titanic* across the Atlantic at maximum speed and beat *Olympic*'s best time, which was set over the course of 11 months of passage.

Figure 5.3: Sister ships Titanic *and* Olympic *seen together for the last time.*

The lesson from this for IT projects today is that business pressures should not override critical operational procedures without some sort of risk assessment.

On leaving Southampton, *Titanic* had a near collision with the steamer *New York* as it broke its mooring and was within four feet of colliding with *Titanic* (Figures 5.4 and 5.5). This was very similar to the incident where *Olympic* collided with *Hawke,* and this illustrates the challenges the crew faced in operating such a large ship.

On reaching Queenstown, in Ireland, the last port before the main Atlantic crossing, the Board of Trade inspected *Titanic*. As part of the inspection, officers

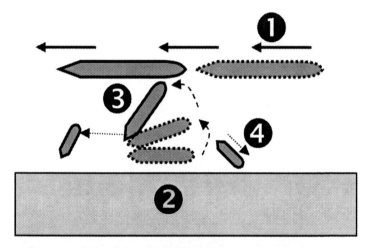

Figure 5.4: Titanic *and* New York *nearly collide.* Titanic *(1) drags* New York *(2) off its mooring, breaking retaining ropes.* New York *(3) comes within four feet of colliding with* Titanic. *The tug* Vulcan *(4) prevents a major collision by restraining* New York.

Figure 5.5: A photo of Titanic *and* New York *together.*

determined the seaworthiness of the vessel, checking the
hull, boilers and machinery. They also checked for
provisions, water, fuel and medical stores. They looked over
steerage compartments for light and air, and inspected the
health of both the crew and steerage passengers.

An important part of the inspection was safety. A
lifeboat drill was performed in front of inspectors to
determine the readiness of the crew. During the drill, only
two lifeboats were lowered, but they did not reach the water,
so the test was not fully completed. The drill outlined that it
took 8 to 10 well-trained men to prepare and lower a lifeboat.
The test failed to highlight that the crew was not very well
prepared to handle a disaster requiring the launch of all 16
lifeboats. In fact, there were only 83 mariners in a crew of
900. The remainder either operated a luxury hotel or the
ship's machinery. Following the inspection, *Titanic* received
a report of "seaworthy and ready to sail" from the
Queenstown Board of Trade.

The lesson from this for IT projects today is that the
objective of testing is to bring to light major flaws missed in
the requirements, design and construction stages. This last
test was completely fudged and highlighted the whole

attitude to testing driven by arrogance that nothing could go wrong.

Conclusions

Today, many IT projects severely compromise testing by not taking it seriously enough and bowing to business pressures to get the solution into production quickly. *Titanic*'s owners were very much driven by the pressing economic need to move *Titanic* into service. In reality, *Titanic*'s testing consisted of the maiden voyage across the Atlantic while fully loaded with passengers. This is understandable, considering the huge amounts of capital that had been invested and which remained tied up during construction. But was it acceptable?

The business opportunity was there for another ship, and White Star's overall objective was to have two luxury liners crossing paths on the Atlantic on a scheduled weekly basis. In addition, *Olympic* had been twice unexpectedly out of service for about eight weeks, so *Ismay* was anxious to see *Titanic* move into service as quickly as possible. But at what cost? Ismay wrote out a new SLO for *Titanic* that proved to be crucial in the next part of the story.

CHAPTER SIX

Implementation & Operations

For an IT solution going into production, it is essential that a support environment is in place for monitoring, operating and controlling the solution through a combination of tools, procedures and people. The objectives are to achieve the Service Levels (SLOs) set out in earlier project stages. Typically, this consists of a multi-hierarchical structure built around a "mean-time-to-recovery clock," where the speed of recovery is an essential factor. This is important if the solution is customer facing or mission critical.

A ship's support environment is not much different, and *Titanic*'s had both frontline and secondary support. This included the lookouts in the crow's nest, the on-duty officers, and the crew on the bridge. The radio operators in the wireless room, analogous to a help desk, communicated with the outside world, controlling the flow of information to and from the ship. Secondary support staff included the safety officer (plotting positions of icebergs, currents and weather systems), the navigation officer (plotting the position of the ship and maintaining the course) and specialized technical positions (like the carpenter, and ship's doctor). The tertiary level of support was provided by the first and second officers, and the captain.

Likewise, IT projects need a similar three-tier support structure for the incoming IT solution. Such a structure is typically made up of operations/help desk, technical and specialist support, operations leaders, and managers.

As *Titanic* left Queenstown, Ireland on April 11, the captain and officers were fully aware of the iceberg dangers ahead. The winter of 1912 had been exceptionally mild, and many icebergs had broken loose. White Star had taken preventative actions prior to the voyage and had re-routed the ship a further 10 miles south. However, this had little effect on Bruce Ismay who was going to race *Titanic* across the North Atlantic. He was confident not only in the ship's safety systems but also in the ship's operation, and the early warning systems in place. *Titanic* had built-in feedback mechanisms for warning the officers and crew of changes in the surrounding environment. These included visual monitoring from the crow's nest and bridge, and ice warnings from other ships in the vicinity. As far as Ismay was concerned, these systems would provide enough warning to take evasive actions.

Today's IT environments leverage built-in feedback mechanisms as part of their support structure to forewarn operations of impending problems. These systems collect data and are programmed to sense "events" or "warnings" that trigger rules-based software and alert operations personnel.

Over the next two-days, *Titanic* received eight warnings reporting ice, icebergs and icefloes. The radio operators, however, only sporadically relayed these ice-warnings to the bridge because they were preoccupied with the flood of outgoing commercial radio messages. The operators were employed by Marconi and paid to transmit commercial radio messages for wealthy first-class passengers sending messages to friends in New York.

This is an important lesson for today's IT projects: all support staff, especially operations, should be given incentive to focus on what is important, like Service Level Agreements, especially when third parties or outsourcers are involved.

The captain and officers were now aware of the fate of the French liner *Niagara* that had struck ice in "iceberg alley" (Figure 6.1) on April 11. But with crossing times, captains were expected by the paying passengers and public to press on and meet the published schedule, very much like airlines today. During the voyage, Captain Smith delayed the mid-Atlantic turn to take a more southerly course by 30 minutes.

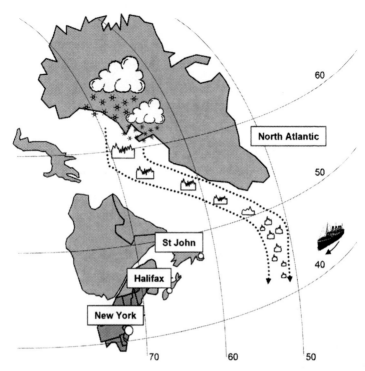

Figure 6.1: In the notorious "iceberg alley," ice flows down from Greenland on well-established currents in often dense formations.

One passenger, Mrs. Ryerson, was concerned over getting to New York one day early and finding a hotel room. She asked Bruce Ismay if the ship would be slowed down as it coursed through the ice field. Ismay is said to have replied, "Oh no, we will put on more boilers to get out of it." He later denied the story at the U.S. inquiry, but fireman Frederick Barrett disclosed that on April 14, three additional boilers had been lit, more than at any other time in the journey, and the ship reached its peak speed. Ismay was risking the ship's safety by forcing it at top speed into the treacherous iceberg alley.

The lesson for today's IT projects is that a business executive should not have the mandate to make operational decisions without the involvement or consent of the operations team.

CHAPTER SEVEN

Common Implementation Mistakes

On the night of April 14, the ship *California* was north of *Titanic*, bound for Boston. After a near-fatal collision with an ice shelf, Captain Stanley Lord decided against proceeding forward and pulled up for the night. Surrounded by pack ice but in no danger, radio operator Evans, under orders from the captain, sent an ice warning to *Titanic*'s radio operators, who had been working a 14-hour day sending/receiving commercial traffic. *Titanic* responded with the infamous, "Shut up, shut up, I am busy. I am working Cape Race and you are jamming me."

This last warning was not passed back to the bridge because of the message overload. The procedure for passing messages back to the bridge was confusing at best. Evans did not try again, turned off his wireless and went to bed.

The lesson from this for IT projects today is that any external warnings from customers or suppliers need to be taken seriously, and to be thoroughly investigated. Finding the meaningful information in a "sea of noise," or redundant information, is invaluable. With *Titanic*, if someone had pieced together all the ice-warning information, it would have indicated a giant ice field around 80 miles wide, directly ahead. Effectively, there was no macro view of the environment.

Any experienced mariner would recognize sea conditions indicative of ice fields. The sea is calmer, as the ice floes and pack ice dampen water movement. The seawater also takes on an oily appearance as it approaches freezing point. The overall visible distance that objects could be seen from the ship was thought to be beyond the norm. This gave the crew a high level of confidence, in being able to spot all hazards. Although stars brightly illuminated the sky and the sea was incredibly calm, there was a haze on the horizon created by the cold weather. This made it difficult to outline the horizon as it merged with the sky.

Titanic had some built-in visual monitoring through the crow's nest and the bridge. Beyond the two lookouts in the crow's nest, officer Lightholler maintained a lookout himself from the bridge. *Titanic* carried six specialist lookouts, and the next shift change was due to start at midnight. A question remains why no extra lookouts were on duty, given all the warning signs. It was typical to post extra lookouts on the bow of the ship, to which a telephone link ran from the bridge. This is another example of the overconfidence of the officers.

The lesson for today's IT projects is that there are critical periods in the business cycle were conditions change, like month end processing, and this requires extra diligence. Unusually quiet conditions should not be taken lightly.

Titanic's lookouts were missing binoculars, which was very unusual. It was customary to always have at least one pair in the crow's nest. The lookouts had repeatedly reported this since leaving Southampton. They were resentful at not having these since they were the tools of the trade required to make them effective. Explanations varied from the statement that they were assigned to officers on the bridge to the speculation that someone stowed them away and was unable to find them in such a large ship.

The lesson for today's IT projects is that certain staff in critical positions, like operations, should have the best equipment available, in preference to others in the hierarchy.

Figure 7.1: A short while after the Titanic sunk, an investigating ship found this iceberg with paint chips on it that matched Titanic.

The temperature of water is a very accurate guide to the proximity of ice in the water. Normally, when entering ice fields, tests were taken by drawing seawater from over the side of the ship with a canvas bucket, and then placing a thermometer in the bucket. Repeated every two hours, these tests were an accurate indicator of the proximity of large ice floes. However, one of the passengers noticed a sailor filling the bucket with tap water because the rope was not long enough to reach the sea.

The lesson for today's IT projects is to investigate feedback mechanisms that are reporting data contrary to other data collected. In *Titanic*'s story, the mechanism was faulty but rather than report the problem the data was falsified to cover it up. It also emphasizes the importance of testing all feedback mechanisms and operational procedures before implementation.

No attempt was made to slow the ship down, despite all the aforementioned warnings. In hindsight, the captain and officers should have done more to clarify the scope of anomalies brought to their attention, investigate them more closely, and piece together all the intelligence. However, no one expected icebergs to be directly in the path of the ship so soon in the voyage, as icebergs did not usually drift down as far south as *Titanic*'s course. The officers must have perceived that anything would be seen well in time with such "excellent" visibility.

Conclusions

Today, many IT projects severely compromise implementation by not taking it seriously enough and bowing to business pressures to get the solution into production quickly. *Titanic*'s owners were very much driven by the pressing economic need to move *Titanic* into service.

In reality, *Titanic*'s testing consisted of the maiden voyage across the Atlantic fully loaded with passengers. This is understandable, considering the huge amounts of capital that had been invested during construction. But was it acceptable? The business opportunity was there for another ship (*Olympic*) and White Star's overall objective was to have two luxury liners crossing paths on the Atlantic on a scheduled weekly basis. In addition, *Olympic* had been twice unexpectedly out of service for about eight weeks, so Ismay was anxious to see *Titanic* move into service as quickly as possible. But at what cost? Ismay wrote out a new SLO for *Titanic* that proved to be crucial in the next part of the story.

CHAPTER EIGHT

Operations

Titanic's early warning system had failed because of the failure to report problems with key feedback mechanisms, possibly because of the fear of reprisal. This, coupled with general over-confidence in the safety of the ship, apathy to the fate of the French liner *Niagara*, and inaccurate information on the extent of the giant ice field led to a state of gross indifference. Finally, Ismay's pressure and new SLO pushed *Titanic* to her highest speed and past her operational limits.

Titanic was heading for a collision. In fact, it was almost inevitable. The ship, at its maximum speed, raced through icy still waters littered with small bergs and pieces of ice. The lookouts, without binoculars and a freezing wind hitting their eyes, were trying to outline the horizon through the haze common in these conditions. As they struggled to make out the shape of a dark mass looming in front of them they delayed reporting this to the bridge.

The lesson for today's IT projects is that in monitoring a newly operational solution, operations staff needs to be very familiar with it. They need to be in a position to proactively prevent failures from happening in the first place and to ensure the solution meets its service levels. They need good visibility into the solution and the surrounding environment. They need to be able to quickly assess and analyze data in front of them, collected from feedback mechanisms set up during the planned testing stage of the project. As the mechanisms become noisy they need to diagnose situations and determine deviations from set norms, any potential impacts, and overall extent. They need to clarify whether there is something actually wrong or just problematic. They need to make the right decision as to whether to escalate, and at what priority.

Titanic's lookouts determined the dark mass was in fact a "growler," or "black iceberg"—an iceberg that has flipped over and is dark in color. With a calm sea and no breakers against the base of the growler it was practically invisible in the haze. This had now turned into a critical situation. Once sure of their sighting they notified the bridge with the infamous "Iceberg dead ahead!" Officer Murdoch, chief duty officer, calmly took the call and with his binoculars confirmed the sighting about 900 yards ahead. From all the evidence available today, Murdoch took the following actions:

- First, he cut power to the engines. This made sense as putting the engines into reverse would just churn up the water and limit the steering and handling capability of the ship.
- Second, there was not enough distance to stop the ship and he could not get around the iceberg. So he attempted a port-around or an S-turn first steering hard a port, and then hard a starboard in an effort to sharply decelerate the ship (Figure 8.1). With only 40 seconds of reaction time this would bring him parallel to the iceberg rather than a head on collision.

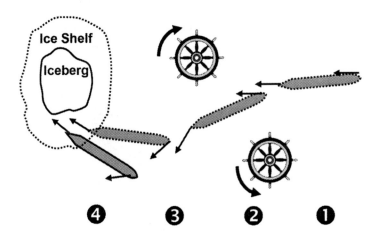

Figure 8.1: Murdoch's course of action was to port around the iceberg. At (1), Murdoch throws the wheel hard to starboard, moving the ship left. At (2), the bow slowly reacts and moves left, while the stern continues forward. At (3), Murdoch throws the wheel hard to port, moving the wheel right. At (4), the bow slowly reacts and moves right while the stern continues moving left, away from the iceberg. The bow runs aground on the underwater ice shelf and the ship grinds to a halt.

- Third, he threw the electric switch to close bulkhead watertight doors (Figure 8.2) as a precaution.

    In hindsight these were probably the best possible actions.

Figure 8.2: The watertight doors seal off compartments in case of an emergency, preventing flooding across multiple compartments.

The lesson for today's IT projects is that in a critical situation, any anomalies spotted are enacted on with a smooth escalation between operations (lookouts) and the levels of technical support staff (bridge officers). This trouble-free escalation needs to be established in the project testing stage and verified through operability and operational testing. As operations become familiar with the solution and environment they set up more effective procedures.

At this point it is evident that there were serious deficiencies in *Titanic*'s project itself. For example, time set aside for testing was too short, the officers did not go through any S-turn maneuvers during sea trials, did not simulate handling the ship under rough or dire conditions, and did not simulate an emergency situation as part of accident prevention.

The lesson for today's IT projects is that operation and technical support staff need time to map out critical scenarios for the operability of the solution, work out strategies for failure prevention, and determine preset and proven courses of action. These need to be carefully carried out and tested prior to implementation. This includes considering automated operators which need to be overridden, otherwise they could cause more problems in a critical situation. After all, the ultimate goal is preventing an outage from occurring, or loss of service, in the first place.

As *Titanic* swung back to starboard, Murdoch just failed to clear the iceberg and he and the bridge staff braced themselves for a collision.

Conclusions

Today, many IT projects severely compromise the operations stage by not paying enough attention to it. Setting up operations is an afterthought and staff are not brought into the project until implementation, rather than taking a prominent role in the planning and testing stages. After all, operations staff are ultimately responsible for upholding the service levels of the solution to the business. The inability to set up an adequate operation (people, processes, tools) around a solution in the first place will inevitably lead to operational problems that manifest themselves days, weeks, or even months after going live, and a potential failure or outage.

Titanic's support staff had little time to familiarize themselves with the ship. They had failed to clarify the scope of anomalies and put together the intelligence. Murdoch's maneuver was well executed, but perhaps with some testing he could have pulled it off better. The friction between operations and technical support over the missing binoculars did not help in the situation and the lookouts hesitation cost vital seconds.

CHAPTER NINE

How a Manageable Situation Turned Worse

T itanic's officers tried desperately to avoid a collision; however, the S-turn, a good decision, failed to decelerate the ship enough. *Titanic* came to a halt later described by hundreds of passengers as a quiver, rumble, or grinding noise that lasted a few seconds, as if the ship was rolling over a thousand marbles.

There was no "crash stop," fatalities, or even minor injuries. There was no violent jolt sideways or repeated strikes along the ship's length. This is common with a side swipe against an ice spur when a ship is turning very hard away from it. The breakfast cutlery that was laid out in the dining salons barely trembled, and drinks remained unspilled in the first class smoking rooms and lounges. All the evidence indicates that the ship came to rest on an underwater ice shelf at the base of the iceberg. Murdoch had prevented a head on crash that could have demolished the first four compartments, and killed or maimed hundreds of passengers.

Likewise, when an IT solution falters in production, steps are taken according to a process prepared, planned, and tested in the project itself. The process should be based around a Mean Time To Recovery (MTTR) clock (Figure 9.1) where the principal objective is to get the IT solution back on-line as quickly as possible to meet Service Level

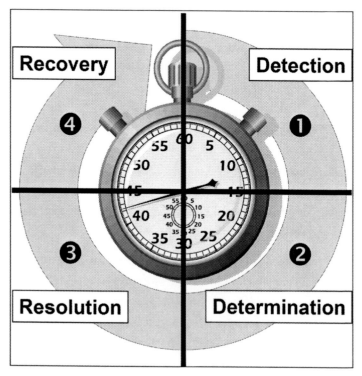

Figure 9.1: The four problem-recovery quadrants of detection, determination, resolution, and recovery.

Agreements (SLAs). The solution is then patched up in the background and a temporary or permanent fix applied; however, before going on-line, the integrity of the solution needs to be first established so that the problem does not reoccur. With an eye on the clock, the operations group steps through the process and the four "problem" quadrants of detection, determination, resolution and recovery (Figure 9.1). When the MTTR clock starts ticking, signifying the beginning of loss of service, metrics should be captured as User Outage Minutes (UOMs) that measure how many users experience service loss and for how long.

Using UOMs is far more accurate than measuring with the more commonly used percentage of service availability, e.g., 99.999 percent. Problem detection on *Titanic* was 37 seconds of warning given by the lookouts. This is not typical with an IT solution, which is likely to put out errors and warnings well before any significant failure occurs. This provides operators, automated or human, time to prevent the problem from occurring in the first place.

Titanic's captain, director, and officers gathered on the bridge (Figure 9.2) to determine a course of action. As part of problem determination to the extent of the damage, two search parties were dispatched into the bowels of the ship: front and mid-ship. The first party returned within 10 minutes with a positive report of no major damage or flooding. In director Bruce Ismay's mind, problem detection and determination were now complete. Resolution with a distress call was a problem for him as it would compromise White Star's position by shattering the hype around *Titanic*

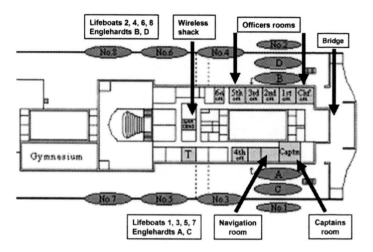

Figure 9.2: In this layout of Titanic's *top deck and bridge, note the ease of access to the bridge or control center from the captain's and officers' quarters. The navigation room is next to the captain's quarters.*

and destroy the brilliant marketing that had lured the world's wealthy elite onto the safest liner ever built.

A better resolution would be to get the ship back to Halifax, away from New York and the center of the world's press. He could then better contain the news story, and marginalize it as a minor incident. He would be able to disembark passengers onto trains, patch the ship up and sail her back to Belfast for repairs. In fact, he could boldly claim that *Titanic*, a lifeboat in itself with all the latest in emerging technologies, was able to save herself from a potential disaster and further push the safety claims of White Star lines.

With an IT solution today, problem determination assesses the impact of the solution on users. Determination has to be consistent with the available evidence. Reinvestigation of feedback mechanisms and logs is vital to determine if the problem has been building up and what has caused it.

In a complex IT solution, it is common to see the domino effect, where a small faulty element like a subsystem knocks out elements around it and triggers a cascade of problems. Not working out this precise sequence of events could lead to a misdiagnosis where a wrong fix is applied and the problem reoccurs. Determination is completed when the root cause assumptions of the problem are tested and proven to be correct.

- With an IT solution, it is important to be sure of the evidence at hand and to ask the following questions:

- Was the IT solution aware it was going to fail? If so, were any (automated) preventative actions attempted?

- Did the solution alert human or automated operators?

- Were any of the feedback mechanisms faulty and provide unreliable data?

- Is the diagnosis of the problem correct?

Titanic's situation was critical, but not catastrophic. Ismay was hell bent on saving face, and his anxiety over White Star's reputation created an atmosphere where mistakes were easily made. *Titanic* appeared to be completely stable, sitting snugly on the underwater ice shelf. Maybe with due care they could dislodge the ship with a minimum of damage. Ismay rushed into making a decision. The second search party with the architect and carpenter had not even returned with an assessment.

The lesson from this for IT projects today is that in resolving the problem it is important to consider the alternative courses of action available, along with the risk associated with each action based on all the collected evidence. Only then should the last quadrant of recovery commence. This is where the operations group puts the IT solution back on-line and resumes services, according to SLAs.

On *Titanic*, not all courses of action were adequately explored as part of the problem resolution. Ismay made the fateful decision to sail forward and telegraphed the engine room "dead slow ahead" to recover the situation. Engineers later testified the ship moved forward at 3 knots with a grinding noise (Figure 9.3).

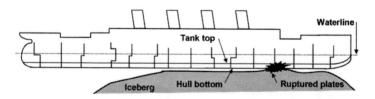

Figure 9.3: Titanic grinds to a stop on the iceberg shelf, which had ruptured the hull bottom and tank top. The flooding was contained by the water pumps.

Conclusions

Today, many IT projects severely compromise the operation stage by not planning adequately in the project for a process to deal with problems around a MTTR clock. Having a process is critical for enabling the operations group to quickly restore service and maintain service levels. A process should also carry the checks and balances (through reviews) to minimize the likelihood of mistakes made in a pressure situation. A process should outline responsibilities and roles to ensure the right personnel make the right decisions.

CHAPTER TEN

How Officers Reacted

Following the collision, the ship appeared to be in remarkably good shape. No one had been injured, and from the bridge the integrity of the ship appeared to be sound. At 11:50 p.m., 10 minutes after the collision, Ismay pushed to restart the ship and limp *Titanic* off the ice shelf. Passengers, unaware of any dangers, later testified their initial relief that the ship was restarting the journey again, with little concern about the collision, the potential damage, and any consequences.

Before a resolution or fix is applied into production, the team needs to assess the overall risk of proceeding with it. Executive intervention is handled like any other input and needs to stand up to careful examination so as not to further deteriorate the situation. Importantly, it needs to be challenged without any repercussions if it does not make sense.

Whether Captain Smith was part of the decision to restart *Titanic* was not really relevant as Ismay was in control of the situation driving forward his own agenda. Smith proceeded to the wireless room to inform the White Star Line in Boston of the situation. Smith was still optimistic; after all, there was a great confidence in the design of the ship with the 73 water tight compartments. Smith sent a wireless message outlining that *Titanic* had struck ice but with little damage. Everyone was safe aboard, and as a precaution the ship was proceeding to Halifax. The message would give White Star time to organize trains and carriages to transport the passengers to New York. Wireless messages were not encrypted and this one was intercepted by the world media. This was the reason why early reports of the collision that appeared in the European press were overwhelmingly optimistic.

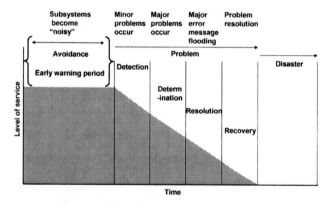

Figure 10.1: The first period in the graph is an early warning period. This is an extremely important mechanism for problem avoidance.

In today's IT projects, MTTR procedures need to be completely controlled by the groups responsible for the IT solution and the services it provides. Communications or announcements related to an outage situation need to be made in close conjunction with these groups and the support decisions they have made when communicating externally to the service recipients. Inaccurate information can quickly erode confidence in the service provider.

The second search party, with the architect Thomas Andrews and the carpenter John Hutchinson, returned with a more accurate assessment of the situation and better data. The first search party had not descended enough decks to see the full extent of the damage. Within seconds of the collision, flooding had occurred in the coal bunkers and Boiler Room 5. One of the firemen later testified seeing a gaping hole 2 feet into the floor of the coal bunker. Suction lines were set up right away and the pumping seemed to be coping with the rate of flooding to keep the ship afloat. Andrews knew that if the mail room was lost to flooding, the ship was doomed.

The lesson from this for IT projects today is that in order to pinpoint faults the support team needs a detailed knowledge of the integrated working solution, and the ability to break it down into logical layers and decompose it into a sequence of products and components. It is key that documentation is created at each stage of the project, and then transfered—as knowledge to support staff for later use in the operation.

After restarting the ship, Boiler Room 6 had started to flood. Around 20 minutes later it was apparent that the initial determination was grossly inaccurate, and the fix was not resolving the situation. The mail room was soon lost to flooding. Smith conferred with Andrews and the officers, determining that the ship—sailing now at 8 knots—should come to a gradual stop. The forward motion had taken its toll. The ship had taken on more water resulting in increased flooding that was becoming catastrophic. Other parts of the ship, which were initially unaffected, had started to spring leaks under the strain of the water.

In a MTTR situation where an IT solution falters, it is important to keep assessing and reassessing the environmental data (evidence) and monitoring the environment for any changes. The first fix applied is usually temporary, so as to get the solution online and back into service quickly. It may take hours or even days to get a permanent fix in place. The solution may have to be patched up in the background: code may have to be reworked or a new component integrated into the solution. This then needs to go through rigorous planning and testing before implementing the changes into production using procedures developed during the project; hence, the requirement for a robust change management process and a test/staging environment.

Andrews rightly predicted to Smith that the ship had approximately two hours before foundering. This was a death sentence, and Smith finally recognized the situation as hopeless—not recoverable like it had been right after the collision.

The lesson from this for IT projects today is that MTTR procedures are cyclical and allow for several attempts at recovery, within a limited time frame. However, Ismay forced a situation where the ship went beyond MTTR or recovery.

Conclusions

Today, many IT projects severely compromise a critical situation by not following an established process in the operation and recovery of a solution. Institutionalized MTTR procedures should help minimize disparate decision making as carried out on *Titanic* and prevent a critical situation from becoming catastrophic. Making sure to use the support staff's detailed knowledge of the solution will also help to reduce the risk of a faulty recovery.

CHAPTER ELEVEN

Disaster Recovery Planning

In recapping *Titanic*'s situation, following the collision the ship was restarted and limped off the ice shelf with the objective of sailing to Halifax. Everything appeared to be in good shape but after 20 minutes of sailing at 8 knots it was apparent that the initial determination was grossly inaccurate. The forward motion had taken its toll and the ship had taken on more water. Parts of the ship initially unaffected had started to spring leaks and the increase in flooding was becoming catastrophic.

In today's world, getting service back online is a top priority, and we often apply a temporary fix whilst a permanent fix is created. However, in such a situation, it is essential that the service delivery environment is closely monitored to determine whether or not the fix is holding.

The second search party, led by the architect Thomas Andrews and the carpenter John Hutchinson, reported major flooding in five compartments and recognized that *Titanic* was not designed for this. The grinding along the bottom had badly ruptured the outer skin and damaged the double hull. The different rates of flooding in the six primary compartments indicated the top hull (or tank top) was damaged. It was beyond the expectations of the designer that something in nature could inflict so much damage.

In today's IT projects, it is vital that a project team plan for such an eventuality, where the fix is not resolving the problem and the situation goes beyond the Mean Time To Recovery. The service is unavailable to end-users and customers and is not readily recoverable any more. For this situation, disaster recovery procedures need to be set up, prepared, planned, and tested by the project team, and institutionalized with the operations or technical support staff.

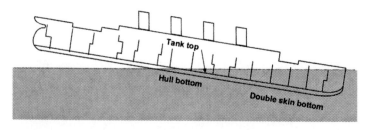

Figure 11.1: All the ship's safety functions failed, except for the lifeboats, as water spilled over the bulkheads from compartment to compartment. This was a major compromise in the bulkheads as a safety feature.

The architect realized the situation onboard *Titanic* had gone beyond normal problem recovery and had become a disaster. He stated that the ship had 2.5 to 3 hours before completely sinking, and accurately determined that the problem could not be fixed. Too many compartments were ruptured and were rapidly flooding beyond the capacity of all the pumps. The bulkhead walls, separating the compartments, had not been carried up to watertight horizontal traverses. Therefore, as the ship's nose went down, water spilled from one compartment to another rather like an ice cube tray filling with water. The ballroom acted as massive channel for distributing water horizontally across the ship (Figure 11.1).

At this point in the story, we see how the compromises to the non-functional requirements during the construction phase of the project had a massive consequence in the disaster.

Only the captain and a few officers knew the extent of the damage and were now resigned to the ship sinking. No "abandon ship" command or formal declaration of a disaster was given. Around 65 minutes after the collision the captain just gave orders to the officers to uncover the lifeboats and get the passengers and crew ready on deck. No formalized disaster recovery plan was in place on board *Titanic*.

In today's world, the next step would be to invoke a disaster recovery plan and communicate it to all onboard. Every disaster recovery plan needs to be accompanied with a well-thought-out communication plan. Such a plan needs to clearly communicate with different audiences.

Titanic's captain understood the seriousness of the situation relatively quickly after the collision, but did not communicate this through the ranks of crew and passengers on board. This increased the confusion, particularly within the crew. For example, the engine room sent some engineers to the boat deck, but the bridge sent them back down to the engine room. There are number of possible explanations for the poor communication aboard *Titanic*:

- The ship had very limited communication capabilities, with no public-address system. Important information was communicated to passengers by word of mouth, the crew knocking on each cabin door, and making announcements in the common rooms. Considering there were hundreds of cabins, this would have taken hours.

- The crew didn't have accurate information on the situation, so varying degrees of information were passed to passengers. The experienced captain believed in the safety systems of the ship and might have found the architect's verdict very hard to accept because everything appeared so normal in the first hour. The captain acted almost as if the situation was "business as usual."

- The captain realized that the carrying capacity of the lifeboats was inadequate, with only enough room for about half of the estimated 2,223 people on board. There were no mass communications in order to keep things calm and to allow the lifeboats to be filled in an orderly manner when the timing was right. The ship's hierarchical structure and segregation of classes meant that first-class passengers had the best access to the boats.

- The captain feared widespread panic. He and the other officers were aware of what had happened aboard the French liner *La Bourgogne* that sank 14 years earlier. With room in the lifeboats for only half the people onboard, widespread panic had broken out. Captain Smith knew he could save the maximum number of lives by loading only those who were lucky enough to reach the boats. So, he may have avoided informing all the passengers, specifically those in third class.

In today's world, a communication plan is probably as important as a disaster recovery plan, for several reasons:

- Communicating internally with your employees can greatly help control the impact of a disaster. Also, the speed of communication is essential. For example, get information to customer-facing employees first, so they can inform customers.
- Communicating externally with your customers is essential and the plan needs to cater to customer segments using different channels, depending on the scope of the problem or disaster. A customer-retention strategy might need to be offered.
- Communicating with the press may be necessary depending on the severity of the loss of service. This requires the identification of key messages, how these

are communicated, and through what channels. Many companies have been caught off guard when roving reporters trap unaware employees with questions.

Conclusions

Today, many IT projects severely compromise an operation by not preparing for worst-case scenarios. In today's world, MTTR procedures are not enough. Aside from a disaster recovery plan, a well-thought-out communication plan needs to be in place.

CHAPTER TWELVE

Invoking the Disaster Recovery Plan

Disaster recovery is the concept of switching the online operation to an alternate service-delivery environment. However, it takes many shapes and forms, from the relatively simple recovery of data and files from a single application in a timeframe measured in days, to the relatively complex recovery of a complete business operation in a timeframe measured in minutes or hours. A disaster can take three forms, namely: total (absolute and immediate), rapid and imminent, slow and innocuous. When a disaster is recognized, contingency plans should be invoked and a disaster declared.

On board *Titanic*, the disaster was slow and innocuous. Although a full recovery was not feasible anymore, the captain and officers could enact a partial recovery. But without a formalized evacuation or disaster recovery plan, the best they could do was to bring some order to prevent widespread panic and chaos once the disaster signs became more obvious. The envisioned scenario for disaster recovery, at the time of the design, was to transfer passengers through lifeboats to another ship and then deliver them to port. The lifeboats would ferry passengers back and forth to the rescue ship, requiring a much smaller total lifeboat capacity. This scenario was based on the perception that *Titanic* could not possibly sink, but would float in an incapacitated state waiting for help.

In defining a disaster recovery plan, thought needs to be given to all the types of failures that could possibly happen to an IT solution and lead to a disaster. For example:

- Physical faults or failures in the technology

- Design errors that include system or application software design failures and bugs

- Operations errors caused by staff due to accidents, inexperience, lack of due diligence or training, not following procedures, or even malice

Environmental failures can be equally devastating, such as those in power supplies, cooling systems and network connections—as can natural disasters and terrorist activities against the operations center itself.

In the past 400 years, most environmental factors related to crossing the Atlantic had been observed, charted and documented. This included year-round natural conditions like changing ocean currents and weather patterns like storms and hurricanes; natural hazards like fogbanks, ice fields, and iceberg areas; and dangerous shorelines, rocky outcrops, and similar features. However, a belief had evolved during *Titanic*'s project that anything that nature could hand out could be handled by this enormous iron ship that was practically unsinkable.

In defining a disaster recovery plan, the scale of disaster is important to consider as well. For example, if a relatively minor storm, fire or flood knocks out your online operation, your customers are going to expect some service contingency plan to kick in relatively quickly. In today's world, you need contingency for all of these, even the most catastrophic disasters.

The associated costs of disaster recovery vary, based on the window of recovery (time), the elements of the disaster, and the degree of recovery required. As part of a plan, these costs need to be determined specifically for the IT solution created.

For *Titanic*, under maritime convention there should have been a disaster recovery plan defined for all the above situations. Such a plan would have brought everyone onboard to the lifeboat deck, loaded them into the lifeboats with places to spare, lowered the lifeboats safely, and put them adrift with experienced crews to handle them. The life boat drill in Queenstown should have tested the latter part of the plan.

Many serious problems with a production environment can start so innocuously that, in the first hour, your organization might not even be aware of the problems or their implications. For example, a less-critical part of the IT solution might be "down," so it goes unnoticed. However, because of interdependencies between components and applications, there tends to be a domino effect where very quickly other parts of the IT solution become affected. This can lead to a catastrophic failure in a very short time.

On board *Titanic* there was a major delay in getting the lifeboats down, indicating a hesitation to launch the boats until as late as possible. It is likely the officers reacted slowly for several reasons: the ship was believed to be unsinkable, the gravity of the situation was not apparent, and everything appeared normal at the time. Also, only 83 of the crew of 900 were actual mariners and were familiar with the somewhat complex drill of lowering a 30 foot (65 person) lifeboat 60 feet to the water. There were 16 of these lifeboats in total, plus four smaller collapsible (45 person) lifeboats or "Englehardts."

Conclusions

Today, many IT projects completely ignore disaster recovery as something beyond their scope and as something covered off by a yearly IT planning process. Yet, it is the IT project that determines the business justification and design around the IT solution, and that develops an in-depth understanding of the kind of recovery that is required. Serious thought needs to be given to the consequences of a disaster impacting the IT solution, and this needs to be done early in the project so that adjustments to the overall disaster recovery plan can be made.

CHAPTER THIRTEEN

Disaster Recovery

The crew carried out orders to launch the lifeboats, but for a long time were skeptical that anything serious was going to happen. Most passengers were unaware of the disaster and the lifeboats were filled on a first-come, first-serve basis from the top decks, mainly first- and second-class passengers. Although each lifeboat had a capacity of 65 people, only 27 very reluctant people were lowered in the first one at 12:45, about 65 minutes after the collision.

Clearly, today's businesses cannot afford environmental failures of the scale of *Titanic*. To ensure their continued survival, they must develop business-continuity plans that reduce the risk of environment downtime and the potentially catastrophic loss of services and data. This activity determines how a company will keep functioning until its normal facilities are restored after a disaster.

Business continuity is a holistic approach to disaster recovery that goes beyond just the technology to recover the whole business operation. So as you design the IT solution, you need to pay attention to the business operations and how they would be replicated. This includes the supporting infrastructure of organization, staff, all the processes and procedures, hard copy records and documentation, and physical facilities. It also includes how employees will be contacted, where they will go, and how they will keep doing their jobs.

From the launch of the first lifeboat, *Titanic*'s recovery window was just over one hour, during which it had to get all of the lifeboats (Figure 13.1) filled and lowered, a stretch for the small crew of 83 mariners. However, the disaster was something not envisaged by the architects who believed *Titanic* would just continue to float, which is a strong argument for why a business continuity plan was not developed in the first place.

The disaster recovery time or recovery window determines the disaster costs as revenue loss is usually directly proportional to the recovery time. Your team should assess the downtime cost for the IT solution, and determine whether the business could slip into a serious financial

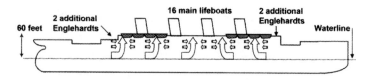

Figure 13.1: The main lifeboats were located on the first-class deck.

situation or bankruptcy. The recovery window is the major variable in disaster planning, and should be based on the maximum window the business can possibly afford.

Onboard *Titanic*, the bridge was the command post. It had remained intact, sustaining no damage. As a result, all major decisions and actions continued to be directed from this location; for example, directing appeals for help through wireless distress calls, slowing down the flooding by shutting watertight doors, and preparing the rockets for firing. At this point, the first of eight distress rockets was fired.

A business continuity plan outlines a disaster recovery method and starts with setting up a command post to direct the recovery operation. This also includes the procedures you should follow for restoring the business services and functions of your IT solution, which can be difficult because of the nuances and anomalies found in business operations. The plan should define responsibilities and guide those executing it.

As the first few lifeboats were lowered, the extent of the damage was still not very visible. The sea was calm, and a slight list of five degrees was not unusual during the crossing. Onboard, the perception existed that the ship could withstand collisions with a dozen icebergs and still remain afloat. Passengers had no preparation for this disaster as no lifeboat drills had been practiced during the voyage. Many passengers arrived on deck, but wandered back to their warm cabins. It took a great deal of persuasion to get the women passengers into the cold lifeboats, leaving their husbands and the warmth of the ship behind. The next three lifeboats left with only 28, 41 and 39 passengers, respectively.

It is important to pay attention to the business procedures around an IT solution. You need to work with individual business functions, groups, and employees to develop contingency plans for each business function. This dramatically increases ownership and familiarity, along with the ability to respond when required by readily enacting the contingency plans.

After 01:00, the warning signs were becoming more obvious. Third-class passengers and stokers who had managed to get up from the decks below had seen the sea water rising up the floors first-hand. They were quite ready to fill the lifeboats. Panic did not break out on *Titanic* however; passengers for the most part filed into the lifeboats in an orderly fashion.

A developed business continuity plan not only lists all the procedures in a "run book" but also the daily activities, tasks, and information flow. It is important to perform a dry run and test the plan to see how people react to it and carry it out. The plan needs to be tested using the same test procedures as used for the IT solution.

Lowering a lifeboat under normal conditions was tricky because of the 60-foot drop. If the lifeboats were overloaded, they could buckle in the middle under the weight. By 01:30, as the ship listed to port the lifeboats on the port side swung away from the ship, and getting into these became hazardous (Figure 13.2). On the starboard side, the lifeboats swung into the ship and bounced along the side of the ship dangerously. There was still hesitation to get in and at 02:00, 140 minutes after the collision, the tenth lifeboat was launched, the only lifeboat that was full.

Figure 13.2: Lowering the lifeboats was challenging as the ship started to list to port, with the uneven flooding of the cells in the double hull.

Without a business continuity plan, recovery is likely to be very poor, especially when dealing with the unexpected. In *Titanic*'s case, these unexpected events include the ship's list and the problems with the launch of the lifeboats.

Conclusions

Today, most IT projects completely overlook business continuity as something beyond the scope of the project. Yet the project is in the best position to identify the business procedures required for the plan. Business continuity can not be an afterthought left until after the project completes.

CHAPTER FOURTEEN

Titanic's Final Minutes

A number of crew (325) and officers (50) remained at their posts, working in holds, boiler rooms, and throughout the ship, ensuring that electricity was available for as long as possible. Consequently, they did not survive. The launch of 16 lifeboats took more than 90 minutes because the order was given late, and the crew was not very familiar with the drill. There was not enough time to properly launch the last two Englehardts (collapsible lifeboats), which were floated off upside-down.

Even if more lifeboats had been available, it is unlikely they would have been launched in the given time. There were only 1,178 lifeboat places and 2,200 people on board. The last 30 minutes were frenetic as most people started to understand th e extent of the disaster. The officers manning the launch of the lifeboats were under a lot of pressure as they controlled an explosive situation. Some scuffles broke out around the last lifeboat and gunshots were heard. In contrast, there were also many heroic acts as some wives refused to be parted from their husbands and get into the lifeboats.

In today's world, a disaster of this proportion can only be mitigated with a business-continuity plan and the appropriate recovery facilities. These should be justified early on in the project, and the design of these should become part of the requirements.

The world press already covering *Titanic*'s maiden voyage was quickly alerted to the ship's situation as can be expected considering the publicity and pomp surrounding the event. The initial reports coming back from the ship were unclear and contradictory. In Europe, the press reflected the initial stages of the disaster and published optimistic accounts that *Titanic* had struck ice but everyone was safe. This is further evidence that the initial on board investigations of the collision were incorrect and that Director Bruce Ismay thought he could limp the ship to Halifax. The first wireless message after the collision was to the White Star office in New York supporting this conclusion. In North America, the press reflected the latter stages of the disaster and published more accurate news, as did later editions in Europe.

In today's world, organizations facing such a disaster would typically go to great lengths to hide these kind of problems away from the media. After all, bad press can destroy reputations and bankrupt a company. In a disaster situation, an organization needs a prepared communication plan to handle all communications between an organization and the outside world, customers and media alike.

A communication plan provides a process for the organization to follow carefully. It is critical in these situations as it helps the organization respond consistently and address what is important in a composed manner. For example, the public relations department would focus on the messages to the media while the chief executives would call key customers.

The temperature of the air was freezing. The sea temperature was actually below the freezing point, and survival time in these temperatures was 20 to 30 minutes. Everything that could possibly float was thrown overboard, in the hopes of use as floating rafts. At 2:20 a.m. on April 15, 1912 the world's largest ship went down to the bottom of the Atlantic. The view from the lifeboats was chaotic.

Initially, the lifeboats had rowed away from the sinking ship for fear of being swamped by survivors in the water. Later, a few of the lifeboats returned to the wreck site before *Carpathia* arrived at 03:30. The lifeboats searched for survivors in the icy water, and amazingly some were found. *Carpathia* had raced at greatest risk through the ice-strewn waters to get there just over an hour after the sinking (Figure 14.1). This was indicative of how much traffic there was in these well-traveled sea lanes of the North Atlantic. It gives some credence to the thinking around the design decisions with the lifeboats, which were perceived as ferrying vessels rather than life-sustaining vessels that could survive open water for several days.

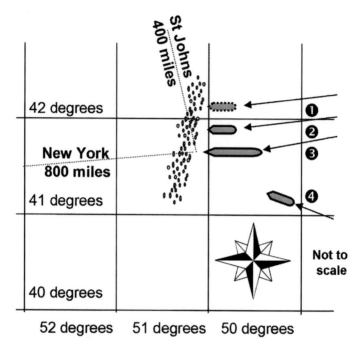

Figure 14.1: Titanic's *disaster and rescue scene outlines the position of the disaster and teh overall directions from which ships came to the rescue: (1)* California's *position as given at the testimony; (2)* California's *likely position; (3)* Titanic's *foundering position; and (4)* Carpathia's *first position, 58 miles away.*

In today's world, an important element of project management is to incorporate lessons learned in future projects. Let's go back to *Titanic* and speculate what could have happened if a disaster-recovery plan was created that had carefully thought out all the possible disaster scenarios. What is important in this exercise is the shift in thinking and the overall process undertaken:

Figure 14.2: Few full lifeboats were lowered to the sea, adding to the number of people who died during the tragedy.

- The first assumption of the White Star planning process would have been the acceptance that the safety systems could possibly fail. This massive shift in thinking would build the plan around evacuating passengers and crew off the ship. This would require enough lifeboat seats for all.

- The second assumption would have centered on how quickly the ship could sink, and therefore the window of evacuation. This would hone the efficiency of the evacuation enacted by the crew within the window. It would require effective lifeboat-launching equipment and a crew trained in its use.

- The third assumption would have considered how quickly a rescue ship could pick up the evacuated passengers and crew from the lifeboats. This would require processes to ensure distress calls were put out quickly. Also, the lifeboats (Figure 14.2) would have to be seaworthy enough to withstand the Atlantic and carry supplies to ensure survival.

Conclusions

Today, many IT projects completely ignore post-implementation elements, such as disaster recovery or business-continuity planning. Yet, if the project team has to consider a recovery/continuity plan early on in the project, it would probably shift the thinking during the design process. The business justification could also factor in the costs of how the IT solution needs to be protected in all circumstances.

CHAPTER FIFTEEN

The Post-Mortem

C*arpathia* arrived at 3:30 a.m. and rescued the lifeboats. She then sailed carefully through the ice strewn waters onto New York without sending any further news. The world was mystified at this remarkable silence. U.S. President Taft's request by wireless for information was unanswered, so he dispatched warships to obtain news. The Navy was unsuccessful and believed that orders were given to *Carpathia* not to answer any queries. On Thursday at 8:30 p.m., *Carpathia* arrived where the world's press awaited her—along with 1,000 relatives and friends of the passengers (Figures 15.1 and 15.2).

In today's world, if you ever face a major operational disaster that impacts your customers, you will have to face the scrutiny of the press and the ire of your customers. For this eventuality, you need a communication plan to handle all communications between your organization and the outside world.

Figure 15.1: The New York Times *ran ongoiung articles on the disaster from when it first happened until the end of the U.S. investigation into the matter.*

Figure 15.2: The world press jumped on the story, and rumours were slowly replaced with details of the tragedy.

Initially, Taft intended to do nothing regarding the disaster. However, the news that the only survivors were those on board the *Carpathia* made the scope of the disaster apparent. The U.S. Senate authorized the Committee on Commerce to investigate the disaster and a hearing was set up with witnesses being subpoenaed. The British Government, worried about an U.S. inquiry that it could not control, quickly followed suit and ordered its own formal inquiry through the Board of Trade (Figure 15.3).

Figure 15.3: Ongoing government investigations on both sides of the Atlantic uncovered details of the disaster that form the basis for this book.

Similarly, following a major unplanned outage you need to go through a post-mortem of your online operation, service-delivery environment, and any recent projects. This will focus the learning energies of your organization on problem prevention, and improve the required levels of service and availability. A post-mortem is an investigation of the sequence of events leading up to a disaster, a major outage, or serious problem. It provides an insight into the factors contributing to the disaster and helps determine the root causes that otherwise would not surface.

A great deal of rivalry existed between the two inquiries as they strived to demonstrate which one was more thorough. The U.S. inquiry started on Friday, April 19 and the British on May 2. This gave the remaining officers time to meet and discuss the sequence of events. The stakes were incredibly high. If the inquiry could find gross negligence in the way the ship was handled, then White Star faced bankruptcy.

There are three steps to take in a post-mortem:

Step 1: The Discovery—This examines what went wrong. What should have/have not happened but did/did not? For this step, you need to collect the evidence (metrics), build the timeline of events, create the problem statement and determine the contributing factors.

Step 2: The Analysis—This examines why it went wrong. What were the contributing factors? What were the root causes of the contributing factors? For this step, you need to categorize the events and analyze the root causes of the events.

Step 3: Corrective Actions—This examines ways to prevent things from going wrong again. For this step, you need to identify corrective actions to root causes, evaluate your organization's support ability and implement the changes.

As part of the first step, a great detail of evidence was collected from *Titanic*'s two investigations. For example, the U.S. inquiry called 82 witnesses within one week of the disaster, including maritime specialists and technical experts. One of the objectives of the U.S. inquiry was to recreate the ship's log through the evidence gathered and to reconstruct the event timeline.

Likewise, you will need to call witnesses and collect as much evidence you can through data and metrics. This needs to be done quickly, as it can get lost—or worse, disappear. Pulling this information together is necessary to create the event timeline.

The U.S. inquiry was worried about losing the opportunity of interviewing witnesses and so had these subpoenaed. Capt. E. J. Smith had gone down with the ship, although his body was never found. Bruce Ismay, the controversial director of White Star who amazingly had survived the disaster, had hoped for a quick return to England. Four officers had survived and were critical witnesses. The surviving crew members (200 out of 700) brought to New York were only paid when they were actually on board a ship, and working. Therefore, they were quite eager to get back to the England and to work.

Two forms of metrics contribute to the event timeline: hard (or quantitative) and soft (or qualitative) metrics. These can be internal or external to an organization. The operational logs in your service-delivery environment highlight the sequence of events and are probably the most important piece of documentation. Typically, these are handwritten, but can be supplemented through the use of automated tools. Other useful documents include operational run books, end-of-shift reports, standard operating procedures, and procedures related to the project.

Hard metrics are system-generated and are collected through manual or automated processes. Examples include reports, error messages, transactions, and statistics. To uncover this data requires on-site "archaeology." These metrics tend to be explicit, time-stamped and accurate, but they usually require aggregation. Reports for these metrics include operational logs, service problem reports, service change requests, service level reports, environmental metric reports, and service outage reports.

Soft metrics include input from employees, project team members, witnesses, customers, and independent bodies. These are solicited through interviews, meetings and workshops. Soft metrics tend to be subjective, difficult to collect, and prone to error, but they can be very insightful to root causes. They can be collected as witness testimonies, employee feed-back, customer feedback, intermediary feedback, marketing feedback, and market perceptions of organization and services. The significance of all these metrics is that they can very accurately help piece together the event timeline.

Conclusions

When projects fail catastrophically, a post-mortem is essential to provide a better understanding of the reason behind the failure. Every IT organization needs to have a post-mortem process in place so little time is wasted in the analysis of the outage. *Titanic*'s inquiries started within a week of the disaster when the evidence was still fresh, and this provides us the greatest body of evidence today. Regardless of whether or not a disaster exists, every project should go through a post-mortem once the solution has been placed in operation to capture any lessons learned during the process.

Titanic Lessons for IT Projects

CHAPTER SIXTEEN

Was There a Conspiracy?

Having collected all the possible evidence, in the form of metrics, the U.S. inquiry proceeded to reconstruct the event timeline right up to the point of impact and beyond. It was and still is standard naval practice to keep a running "ship's log" on board a ship that is documentation of all sea and weather conditions, and all events carefully recorded, for all eventualities such as an inquiry.

In today's world this is still the first step of a post-mortem; namely, the discovery of what went wrong, and what should have or should not have happened. For this step, you need to collect the evidence (metrics) and build the timeline of events.

One of the challenges for the U.S. inquiry was the ability to detain witnesses for a prolonged length of time. Specifically, the British crew of White Star employees, who had to be subpoenaed, received no salary when on shore in New York. Therefore, the U.S. inquiry had to get to the root cause quickly and gather information. This was a problem as some information would only reveal itself after several interviews. Other information would seem irrelevant at first but become essential once patterns emerged.

In the U.S. inquiry the following expert testimonies were identified:

"My theory would be that she was going along and touched one of those large spurs from an iceberg. There are spurs projecting out beneath the water, and they are very sharp and pointed."
(Extract from the testimony of Capt. James Henry Moore)

This set up the myth that it was a hard collision. In contrast the following passenger and crew testimonies of the collision were identified:

"I heard this thump, then I could feel the boat quiver and could feel a sort of rumbling."
(Joseph Scarott, Seaman)

"... It was like a heavy vibration. It was not a violent shock."
(Walter Brice, Able Bodied Seaman)

"...I felt as though a heavy wave had struck our ship. She quivered under it somewhat."
(Major Arthur Peuchen, First Class Passenger)

"I was dreaming, and I woke up when I heard a slight crash. I paid no attention to it until the engines stop."
(C E Henry Stengel, First Class Passenger)

"We were thrown from the bench on which we were sitting. The shock was accompanied by a grinding noise...."
(Edward Dorking, Third Class Passenger)

"It was like thunder, the roar of thunder..."
(George Beauchamp, Fireman)

A collision at 24 knots with a spur of ice would have been a "hard collision" and knocked everything sideways resulting in many casualties with broken limbs. There is overwhelming testimonial evidence that this was a "soft collision" where the breakfast cutlery barely rattled.

The final report described the collision as:

"The impact, while nonviolent enough to disturb the passengers or crew, or to rest the ship's progress, rolled the vessel slightly and tore the still plating above the turn of the bilge."

This infers a sideswipe of a spur which has become one of the myths around *Titanic*.

The U.S. inquiry succeeded in identifying critical information; for example, the ship had reached a peak speed just prior to the collision, Director Bruce Ismay was interfering with the command of the ship, and that the basic feedback mechanisms were compromised. However, the U.S. inquiry captured but failed to explain the following discrepancies:

- The testimony of Quatermaster Oliver indicated that Captain Smith rang down to the engine room "Ahead slow" 10 minutes after the grounding, moving the ship forward.

- Senator Alden Smith discovered White Star had dispatched trains to Halifax, but these were cancelled well after the ship had foundered.

Other evidence:

- Wireless Radio Operator Philips sent a message to his parents 12 minutes after the grounding "Making slowly for Halifax. Practically unsinkable. Don't worry." This was further evidence that the ship was moving after the grounding.

- The testimonies of officers and key crew members (such as the lookouts) were very specific to the questions asked, and none offered anything more than was asked. It is apparent that they were well-prepared as witnesses or coached into how to avoid saying anything damaging.

The cover up over the grounding on the ice shelf and sailing off was not uncovered by the U.S. inquiry. Although it did collect the evidence, the inquiry failed to piece it together. Had it done so, the inquiry would have produced different conclusions.

Continuing with your Post-mortem

In today's world, to complete step one of the post-mortem you need to create a problem statement and determine the contributing factors. To better understand how to proceed with your own post-mortem, this section illustrates what should have been uncovered by the U.S. inquiry into the *Titanic* disaster had the post-mortem process been properly followed.

In a post-mortem, once you have the timeline of events you need to select the events that had the most impact on the disaster—those thought to be "problematic"—before you can start to discover root causes. To select these key events requires careful definition of a problem statement, as there might be ambiguity around which problem are important, or if several problems occurred simultaneously.

For example, for a post-mortem regarding *Titanic*'s disaster a first question about the disaster might have been "Why did *Titanic* not reach New York?" The answer simply is that it ran onto an ice shelf and foundered after it sailed off. However, it is important to phrase the question in a meaningful context to the organization and in this case the tragic and huge loss of life, so that the question should have read "Why was *Titanic* such a tragic disaster, with so many lives lost?" The emphasis should have been on learning lessons and preventing future catastrophes. After all, the public had relatively little sympathy for White Star and its economic loss.

A good problem statement helps determine the contributing factors to *Titanic*'s disaster:

1. Officers failed to slow the ship down and prevent the collision with the ice shelf.

2. The Director and Captain sailed the crippled ship off the ice shelf for Halifax (based on the above discrepancies).

3. Recovery was undertaken poorly by both officers and crew.

In your post-mortem, you are now ready to proceed with a detailed analysis (step two) that will lead you to the root causes of the disaster. This step determines why things went wrong. The first element of this step is to select the events that had the most impact on the disaster, or were most "problematic" related to the contributing factors. For example, for the first contributing factor (Officers Failed to Slow Ship) these were:

a) Seven ice warnings were received during the day, but were only passed on an *ad hoc* basis to bridge.

b) The last ice warning from *Mesba* was not passed to the bridge.

c) Visible signs of ice around the ship were ignored.

d) Lookouts spotted ice looming 50 feet above the water, but could not prevent a collision.

For the second contributing factor (Crippled Ship Was Sailed Off Ice Shelf) the critical events were:

a) Water damage in the fore peak and cargo hold was not taken seriously enough.

b) Bruce Ismay arrived on deck to check damage and assumed authority over the Captain.

c) The first investigation group led by Officer Boxhall returned with an inaccurate damage assessment.

d) The Director and Captain restart the engines acting on sparse information, reluctant to wait for the report of the second investigation group.

For the third contributing factor (Recovery Undertaken Poorly by Officers and Crew) the critical events were:

a) Executives were aware that the ship had few hours left but that information was not widely communicated.

b) No "abandon ship" order was given; the information flow was very slow or even restricted.

c) The first distress call was sent out 40 minutes into the disaster, showing a reluctance to face up to situation.

d) The first distress rocket was sent 65 minutes into disaster, confirming a reluctance to face up to situation.

e) The first few lifeboats left half-empty 65 minutes into the disaster, and the crew could not persuade passengers to board them.

The next step in the post-mortem process is a detailed analysis of the first contributing factor (Officers Failed to Slow Ship):

- A lower speed would have prevented the disaster, an opinion shared by naval architects and engineers. The iceberg's impact would have been minimized, and with less damage to the hull plates, fewer compartments would have flooded.

- The officers were so confident in their ship's handling that, despite numerous warnings, they chose to press full-speed ahead, possibly because:

    a) Of the experience gained with *Olympic*, which had been in operation for 11 months, similar conditions had been encountered.

    b) The built-in feedback mechanisms would provide early warning signs of ice.

    c) Numerous ships sailing along busy sea routes would provide ample radio message warnings of ice.

    d) The visibility conditions were perceived as excellent. The sea was very still and the night sky very clear, so danger should be seen in advance.

The detailed analysis for the second contributing factor (Crippled Ship Was Sailed Off Ice Shelf) showed some interesting causes:

- The Director and Captain, convinced that no serious damage had been sustained, restarted the engines and floated the ship off the ice shelf, with the hope of limping back to Halifax. They chose to do so possibly because:

  a) The collision seemed so innocuous, with no signs of visible damage and no casualties. The impact was no more than a vibration and grinding noise that grounded the ship.

  b) The resounding belief was that the safety features could cope with the damage. The water pumps and double hull were keeping up with the flooding and the bulkheads were sealed.

  c) The first damage-assessment report was incorrect because Officer Boxhall's group did not descend enough decks to properly observe the damage.

  d) The Director and Captain were too impatient for the second damage-assessment report because of business pressure to arrive in Halifax within a specific timeframe to the estimated arrival time. The Director saw an opportunity to extend the legend of Olympic-class ships further, in having the ship save itself. He was under business pressure to maintain the perception that *Titanic* was the greatest liner ever, and to avoid embarrassing publicity if distress calls were put out stating that the ship was grounded on an ice shelf.

The detailed analysis for the third contributing factor (Recovery Undertaken Poorly by Officers and Crew) showed the following items:

- The officers and crew were unable to enact a smooth recovery. The statistics for third-class passengers lost were horrendous compared to the total numbers aboard. Also, had the officers and crew filled the lifeboats, an additional 750 people could have been saved. They chose to do so possibly because:

  a) No business continuity plan was in place, so full recovery was impossible. A plan was thought unnecessary because of the confidence in the ship's safety features.

  b) The crew was preoccupied in helping first-class passengers to the boat deck and life-boats.

  c) The cascading information flow was very slow, and the Captain failed to give concrete orders like "abandon ship." The crew lied to the third-class passengers about the extent of the damage so that they would return to their quarters.

  d) Officers and crew responded slowly because of the disbelief that the ship was in danger, and only realized something was wrong as disaster signs appeared after the first hour. There was an overconfidence in the ship and its safety features.

- Third-class passengers had great difficulty in getting to the boat decks, because:

  a) The class system on the ship exasperated the problem of movement. The lower the class, the further and deeper into the ship was the accommodation.

  b) Third-class passengers were physically restricted by gates and barriers from wandering outside of their class because American immigration regulations specified that immigrants on ships be segregated from other classes, for health reasons.

  c) Many of these gates were locked while the ship sank because the crewmembers in charge of the gates were unavailable.

  d) Many third-class passengers themselves accepted their "lower position" in the socially created hierarchy, which further reinforced the segregation.

In your post-mortem you are now ready to proceed with the third step that tests and rationalizes the root causes into true causes, and determines solutions or corrective actions. The purpose of this step is to prevent the disaster from happening again.

For example, for the first contributing factor (Officers Failed to Slow Ship) the root causes were:

1. Clear procedures were lacking; for example, procedures for passing ice warning messages to the bridge, and for the officers to chart the ice field's size. Had one of the officers been able to put together all the ice warnings, it is very likely the size of the ice field would have been better understood.

2. Business pressure to better *Olympic*'s crossing time influenced action. The Director was determined to prove that *Titanic* was a better ship. Sea conditions were calm and so were treated in a cavalier manner whilst other ships in the region had pulled up for the night.

3. Data from feedback mechanisms was distrusted, discounted, or just ignored by the officers if it didn't fit in with their perceptions. Some data, like the result of the ice-bucket test, were fabricated. The Captain, a technophobe, tended to operate by instinct.

4. Officers saw no reason to post more lookouts to the ship's prow as visibility was perceived to be excellent. In reality, it was very poor because of the haze caused by the cold weather, and with the calm sea there were no breakers to identify icebergs on the horizon. Lookouts were posted without binoculars, while officers kept their own.

The second root cause (above) is likely the true cause of the disaster's first contributing factor. A remedy could have been to play down the significance of the maiden voyage and have a "burn-in period" of shorter trips. Then, later in the summer, when icebergs were less likely, reschedule the voyage and take a more southerly route. However, there were great financial pressures to get *Titanic* operational quickly.

For the second contributing factor (Crippled Ship Was Sailed Off Ice Shelf) the root causes were:

1. Officers and crew disbelieved the seriousness of the situation. Even an hour later, there was still a disbelief in the seriousness of the situation by officers and crew, a common disaster trait.

2. There were strong business pressures to maintain the perception that *Titanic* was the greatest liner ever. The Director callously exploited a very risky opportunity to save face by turning a problematic situation into a positive one, in his mind.

3. The first damage assessment group was not expecting any serious damage. The investigation was hurried and not done thoroughly. The executives were looking for exactly this type of evidence to use to their advantage.

4. Executives could override procedures and the rules of good seamanship. The Director used his position to take control of the operation and all key operational decisions, without adequate relative experience, to the

detriment of the organization. The Captain was intimidated by the Director, even with the overwhelming evidence of the dangers. The overriding authority of the Director, Captain, and the hierarchical culture made it impossible to challenge.

Root causes two and four are likely the true causes of the second contributing factor. A remedy could have been to establish SLAs (to deliver passengers safely) and then establish responsibility firmly with one group alone (operations services) to meet these without any interference from executives whatsoever.

In a critical situation, it is easy to lose control and make rash decisions on too little information. Hence, the group responsible for operations services needs to follow processes such as a problem-management process. It is likely they would have refused to take action before examining more evidence, and the ship could have stabilized on the ice shelf. This would have been long enough for rescue ships to complete a full recovery of the majority of the passengers.

For the third contributing factor (Recovery Undertaken Poorly by Officers and Crew) the root causes were:

1. A fear of widespread panic. This was inevitable, as many of the third-class passengers on the lower decks, where the flooding was most apparent, were well aware of the disaster very early on. In many organizations, outages are first noticed by customers.

2. Communication systems were very poor. The crew had to alert passengers by knocking from door to door, which took up to an hour. On the upper decks, a level of calm was kept, as the crew was close by and helpful, unlike the lower decks, where the signs of disaster were more visible.

3. No business-continuity plan was in place. A disaster-recovery plan had not been carefully thought out for all scenarios.

The third root cause is likely the true cause of the third contributing factor. A remedy could have been to establish a disaster-recovery plan, carefully thought out for all possible scenarios. The plan would be well communicated and regularly practiced.

U. S. Inquiry and Changes to Maritime Transportation

A disaster of *Titanic*'s proportion was probably the only single event that could shake up shipping companies into making changes and introducing safety standards to keep up with changes in emerging technology. The U.S. inquiry led to the following changes:

• The International Conference for the Safety of Life at Sea (SOLAS) approved this following resolution in November 1913: "When ice is reported on or near his course, the Master of every vessel is bound to proceed at night at a moderate speed or to alter his course, so as to go well clear of the danger zone."

- In 1913, the International Ice Patrol organization was created, financed by the nations that used the North Atlantic shipping lanes. The sea lanes were patrolled during the period of greatest iceberg danger, in the January-to-August timeframe.

- The number of lifeboats was increased on ships to "a place for every soul."

- After the sinking, Morse code was installed as the standard communication for ships at sea by most maritime nations. At an international conference, convened three months after the disaster, the SOS distress signal was adopted. The signal was adopted merely because it was an easily recognizable letter sequence of three dots, three dashes, and three dots. However, it became popularly known as "save our souls" or "save our ship."

- The wireless became accepted as an important safety device. Each ship required two radio operators to cover the 24-hour day. No longer was the wireless seen as a tool to entertain passengers.

- The southern Atlantic route was moved even farther south by sixty miles during the summer, to avoid any risk of iceberg collision.

- The German liner *Imperator*, built in 1912 after the disaster, was delayed by the addition of an inner skin, which extended above the water line in the forward compartments. The space between was five feet and was filled with water to test the tightness of the skins.

The British Inquiry

The British investigation was a white-wash. It shifted the blame onto the Board of Trade, for not changing the lifeboat regulations to keep pace with increases in ship size, and the captain of *California*, Captain Stanley Lord, who sat the night out. He was surrounded by ice, unaware of the disaster, and did not come to the rescue of *Titanic*. However, even if *California* had come to the call, it is highly likely that the rescue attempt would have been unsuccessful. The British government needed White Star to stay in business. It saw a potential European war looming, and knew it would need large ships for transporting troops and materials. In today's world, *Titanic*'s disaster would undoubtedly have brought White Star down just through private lawsuits. In the business world, this has repeatedly happened. You need to consider these implications carefully, and their impact when putting your operations on-line.

CHAPTER SEVENTEEN

Conclusion

In reviewing *Titanic's* case study, by the project-construction stage, decisions were made in the architecture and design that compromised and negated principal safety features, like the height of the bulkheads, and the number of lifeboats. The logical explanation is that assumptions were made by the White Star architects, principally that the aggregated effect of the combined safety features and advanced technology incorporated would protect *Titanic*. The arrogant view evolved that *Titanic* was a huge lifeboat. *Titanic's* designers made the mistake of believing the initial design assumptions, not testing these far enough, and not evolving expectations. Such was the confidence in the safety of the ship that by the end of the project disaster recovery and business continuity plans were considered superfluous.

In the early stages of your IT project's lifecycle, architecture and design, hundreds of granular decisions are made by your team. Some of these decisions might seem innocuous or insignificant. As the project takes shape, however, assumptions are formed. It is very easy to stray off the path in one stage and make unsound, dubious decisions but still meet the goal of that stage. For example, underestimating the costs of non-functional requirements is a common problem that must be factored into the business case (as discussed in Chapter 2). The impact of a poor decision might not be brought to light until later in the project, or even months after the operation is on-line.

You need to ensure that your project stays true to its vision and direction through each stage of the lifecycle. It is unfeasible for you to micro-manage the project so you have to ensure that everyone involved understands the project vision clearly, and is empowered to aggregate information, determine risks, and present critical issues at steering-committee meetings. Strategies like starting with a pilot or small project and then scaling each project lifecycle rapidly minimizes the impact of poor decisions.

The belief in *Titanic's* invincibility grew through the sea trials and into the maiden voyage, as the officers and crew went about their duties. By the end of the project, *Titanic* was the largest ship afloat and was billed as unsinkable. Everyone, from the Captain, to the crew, to the 53 millionaires onboard, believed this. White Star did a brilliant job in marketing *Titanic* as the ultimate crossing experience. Why else would the wealthy and powerful have filled the hold and safes with cars and riches, and come aboard on a potentially treacherous route? Fundamentally, they believed that man had conquered nature and there was little risk.

Likewise, your project needs to include careful investment in planning, testing, and operating. It is easy to dismiss these stages in the project lifecycle and accept minimal testing, without realizing that you will pay for it eventually when things do go wrong. On completing your project successfully, it is easy to become very complacent and assume nothing will go wrong. After all, you have invested in the latest mission-critical technology, integrated reliable software, and marketed the solution extensively to your customer base.

The ship owners were very much driven by the pressing economic need to move *Titanic* into service. In reality, *Titanic's* testing consisted of the maiden voyage across the Atlantic, fully loaded with passengers. This was a disaster waiting to happen. The poor operational readiness of the ship, coupled with the cavalier and arrogant attitude of its executives, violated all the basic rules of good seamanship.

Similarly, organizations today make a large number of assumptions that might prove incorrect when implementing operations on-line. Confidence that nothing can go wrong creates an atmosphere where little attention is paid to operational readiness.

Officer Murdoch came close to preventing *Titanic's* initial collision through brilliant seamanship, when he almost pulled off an S-turn. However, he was under tremendous pressure not to slow down, and was forced to navigate a very risky run through a hazardous ice field. The operation of the ship was pushed beyond the limits for which its safety features were designed.

Similarly, it is very easy to attribute major outages or problems in your on-line operation to operator error or even a malfunction with the hardware or software. These explanations are simply not acceptable in today's world, where the stakes are so high. You need to ask why the operator made the error, what sort of pressure the operator was under, why the hardware or software went wrong, and why this was not caught in the testing stage of the project. The root causes to many problems are laid during the on-line operation project.

What You Can Learn from Root Causes

In reviewing *Titanic*'s post-mortem, eleven significant root causes were identified. Nine of these were related to organizational issues, two were related to the lack of procedures or plans, and none were related to technology.

The following four root causes were most significant:

- The business pressures to better *Olympic's* crossing time influenced actions, as the Director was determined to prove *Titanic* was a more technically advanced ship.

- The Director used his authority to take control of the operation and all major decisions, even though stringent guidelines and procedures were in place.

- No business continuity plan was in place, as it was thought unnecessary.

- The business pressure to maintain the perception of the greatest liner ever caused the Director to callously exploit a very risky opportunity to save face.

It is clear that the true causes were related to business pressures overriding operational decisions, and very poor leadership. This is absolutely typical in today's on-line environments, where business pressures and overzealous leadership can override operational decisions. It is essential that you complete post-mortems for all major problems and closely look at the root causes in your on-line operation, and not accept superficial excuses.

In today's popular culture, we have come to accept that *Titanic* was just unlucky. The truth behind the root causes was falsified for political reasons. The failure of White Star's Captain, officers, and crew to protect the ship should have resulted in a case of gross incompetence being brought against White Star. In effect, the British investigation knew that it would have to exonerate White Star to prevent rival German companies from dominating transatlantic shipping.

Photo Credits

Figure 1.1 - The White Star Lines logo. Source unknown.

Figure 1.2 - *Olympic* and *Titanic* in slipways. Courtesy of the Ulster Folk & Transport Museum.

Figure 3.2 - Shipbuilder's model of *Olylmpic* and *Titanic*. Courtesy of the Ulster Folk & Transport Museum.

Figure 3.6 - Onboard sternward view of upper deck and lifeboats. Courtesy of the Ulster Folk & Transport Museum.

Figure 3.7 - Laying the keel of *Titanic*. Courtesy of the Ulster Folk & Transport Museum.

Figure 4.1 - Workers leaving the H&W shipyards. Source unknown.

Figure 4.3 - *Olympic*'s damage from *HMS Hawke* collision. Courtesy of the Ulster Folk & Transport Museum.

Figure 5.1 - Starboard stern view of completed ship in Belfast Lough with tugs. Courtesy of the Ulster Folk & Transport Museum.

Figure 5.2 - Another view of *Olympic*'s damage from collision with *Hawke*. Courtesy of the Ulster Folk & Transport Museum.

Figure 5.3 - *See Figure 1.2.*

Figure 5.5 - *Titanic* and the liner *New York* together. Source unknown.

Figure 7.1 - Suspected iceberg that sunk *Titanic*. Courtesy of the Encylopedia Titanica (www.encyclopedia-titanica.org).

Figure 8.2 - Electric door of *Olympic*. Courtesy of the Ulster Folk & Transport Museum.

Figure 9.2 - The illustration of *Titanic*'s general arrangement plan was used courtesy of the Encylopedia Titanica (www.encyclopedia-titanica.org).

Figure 14.2 - Lifeboat full of people. Source unknown.

Figure 15.1 - *New York Times* cover story of the *Titanic* disaster. Courtesy of the *New York Times* archives .

Figure 15.2 - Newsboy Ned Parfett outside the White Star Line offices at Oceanic House in Cockspur Street, London, S.W., holding an *Evening News* poster announcing "Titanic Disaster Great Loss of Life." Courtesy of the Encylopedia Titanica (www.encyclopedia-titanica.org).

Figure 15.3 - *Titanic* disaster hearings. Source unknown.

Bibliography

1998 MERIT Project. *Best Practices in Enterprise Management.*

Adams, Johnathan; Galambos, George; Koushik, Srinivas; Vasudeva, Guru. *Patterns for e-business: A Strategy for Reuse.* IBM Press.

Bonsall, Thomas E. *Great Shipwrecks of the 20th Century.* New York: Gallery Books.

Bristow, Diana. *Titanic: Sinking the Myths.* KatCo Literary Group of Central California, June 1995.

Brown, David. *The Last Log of the Titanic.* McGraw-Hill.

Davie, Michael. *The Titanic: The Full Story of a Tragedy.* The Bodleyhead Ltd.

Eaton, John P.; Haas, Charles A. *Titanic: Triumph and Tragedy.* Norton, March 1995.

Hyslop, Donald; Forsyth, Alastair; Meminia, Sheila. *Titanic Voices.* New York: St. Martin's Press, 1998.

Kozak-Holland. *On-line, On-time, On-budget: Titanic Lessons for e-business Executives.* Double Oak, TX: IBM Press, 2002.

Lord, Walter. *A Night to Remember.* New York: Holt, Rineheart & Winston, 1955.

Lord, Walter. *The Night Lives On.* New York: Holt, Rinehart & Winston, 1985.

Maxtone-Graham, John. *The Only Way to Cross.* Barnes & Noble Books, 1998.

Spignesi, Stephen. *The Complete Titanic.* Birch Lane Press Group, 1998.

Thompson, Harvey. *Customer Value Management.* McGraw0Hill, 2000.

Wade, Wyn Craig. *The Titanic: End of a Dream.* New York: Rawson-Wade, 1979.

Wels, Susan. *Titanic: Legacy of the World's Greatest Ocean Liner.* Alexandria, VA: Time-Life Books, 2000.

Index

About the Author

Mark Kozak-Holland is a Senior Business Architect/Consultant with HP Services. Mark has many years of international experience working with organizations in formulating projects and initiatives for developing and integrating solutions that leverage emerging technologies. He has been working with mission-critical solutions since 1985.

   In these service delivery environments, great attention is paid to making the solution available continually without having interruptions to service for any reason. As a consultant, Mark was involved in designing and running these solutions. He was also involved in investigating operational failures in these environments. One of the challenges in investigating these types of failures was convincing management that the root causes were in the project itself. As a result, Mark investigated some of the notable disasters of the 20th century and began to research *Titanic* extensively. *Titanic* provided an excellent analogy as to why solutions fail catastrophically when put in operation, literally 4 days into production. The root causes lay in the 4 year construction project itself and the decision making that went on.

Mark is very passionate about history and sees its potential use as an education tool in business today. As a result, he has started to develop a "lesson-from-history" series, which is for organizations applying today's Information Technology (IT) to common business problems. It is written for primarily business and IT professionals looking for inspiration for their projects. It uses relevant historical case studies to examine how historical projects and emerging technologies of the past solved complex problems.

For thousands of years people have been running projects that leveraged emerging technologies of the time, to create unique and wonderful structures like the pyramids, buildings, or bridges. Similarly, people have gone on great expeditions and journeys, and raced their rivals in striving to be first, e.g., circumnavigating the world or conquering the poles. These were all forms of projects that required initiating, planning, executing, controlling and closing.

The series looks at historical projects and then draws comparisons to challenges encountered in today's projects. It outlines the stages involved in delivering a complex project providing a step-by-step guide to the project deliverables. It vividly describes the crucial lessons from historical projects and complements these with some of today's best practices.

It makes the whole learning experience more memorable. The series should inspire the reader as these historical projects were achieved with a less sophisticated emerging technology.

Email: **mark.kozak-holl@sympatico.ca**

Web Sites: **http://www.mmpubs.com/kozak-holland/**
             http://www.lessons-from-history.com/

HISTORY

About the Series

This series is for primarily business and IT professionals looking for inspiration for their projects. Specifically, business managers responsible for solving business problems, or Project Managers (PMs) responsible for delivering business solutions through IT projects.

This series uses relevant historical case studies to examine how historical projects and emerging technologies of the past solved complex problems. It then draws comparisons to challenges encountered in today's IT projects.

This series benefits the reader in several ways:

- It outlines the stages involved in delivering a complex IT project providing a step-by-step guide to the project deliverables.

- It vividly describes the crucial lessons from historical projects and complements these with some of today's best practices.

- It makes the whole learning experience more memorable.

The series should inspire the reader as these historical projects were achieved with a lesser (inferior) technology.

Website: **http://www.lessons-from-history.com/**

If you liked this book, you may also be interested in...

This book analyzes a period of time from World War II when Winston Churchill, one of history's most famous leaders, faced near defeat for the British in the face of sustained German attacks. The book describes the strategies he used to overcome incredible odds and turn the tide on the impending invasion. The historical analysis is done through a modern business and information technology lens, describing Churchill's actions and strategy using modern business tools and techniques. Aimed at business executives, IT managers, and project managers, the book extracts learnings from Churchill's experiences that can be applied to business problems today. Particular themes in the book are knowledge management, information portals, adaptive enterprises, and organizational agility.

ISBN: 1-895186-19-6   (paperback)
ISBN: 1-895186-20-X   (PDF ebook)

http://www.mmpubs.com/churchill

CPSIA information can be obtained at www.ICGtesting.com
Printed in the USA
BVOW061259110412

287363BV00001B/23/A